# ETHERNET TIPS AND TECHNIQUES

## 3RD EDITION

## BYRON L. SPINNEY

To join a Prentice Hall PTR Internet mailing list, point to:
http://www.prenhall.com/mail_lists/

**Prentice Hall PTR**
**Upper Saddle River, NJ 07458**

Editorial/production supervision: *Craig Little*
Cover design director: *Jayne Conte*
Cover design: *Bruce Kenselaar*
Manufacturing manager: *Alexis R. Heydt*
Acquisitions editor: *Mike Meehan*
Marketing manager: *Steve Solomon*

© 1998 Prentice Hall PTR
Prentice-Hall, Inc.
A Simon & Schuster Company
Upper Saddle River, New Jersey 07458

Prentice Hall books are widely used by corporations and government agencies for training, marketing, and resale.

The publisher offers discounts on this book when ordered in bulk quantities. For more information, contact Corporate Sales Department, Phone: 800-382-3419; FAX: 201-236-7141; email: corpsales@prenhall.com
Or write: Prentice Hall PTR, Corporate Sales Dept., One Lake Street,
Upper Saddle River, NJ 07458.

All product names mentioned herein are trademarks of their respective owners.

All rights reserved. No part of this book may be
reproduced, in any form or by any means,
without permission in writing from the publisher.

Printed in the United States of America
10  9  8  7  6  5  4  3  2  1

ISBN 0-13-755950-X

Prentice-Hall International (UK) Limited, *London*
Prentice-Hall of Australia Pty. Limited, *Sydney*
Prentice-Hall Canada Inc., *Toronto*
Prentice-Hall Hispanoamericana, S.A., *Mexico*
Prentice-Hall of India Private Limited, *New Delhi*
Prentice-Hall of Japan, Inc., *Tokyo*
Simon & Schuster Asia Pte. Ltd., *Singapore*
Editora Prentice-Hall do Brasil, Ltda., *Rio de Janeiro*

# Contents

Preface .............................. xvii

**Chapter 1:** **An Introduction to Local Area Networking** .............. 1

    1.1 Local Area Networks ............... 1
    1.2 Brief History .................... 2
        1.2.1 Serial Communications ....... 3
        1.2.2 More Advanced Terminals and Connectivity ................. 4
        1.2.3 Topologies ................. 4
        1.2.4 Ring ....................... 5
        1.2.5 Bus ........................ 6
        1.2.6 Star ....................... 7
        1.2.7 Tree ....................... 8
        1.2.8 Topology Summary .......... 10
    1.3 LAN/WAN ...................... 10
    1.4 ISO/OSI ........................ 11
    1.5 Chapter Summary ................ 13
        1.5.1 Major Concepts ............. 13
    1.6 Vocabulary ..................... 14
    1.7 Chapter 1 Review Questions ........ 15

**Chapter 2:** **Introduction to Ethernet** ...... 17

    2.1 Introduction .................... 17
    2.2 A Brief History .................. 18
    2.3 What Is Ethernet? ................ 19

## CONTENTS

|  |  |
|---|---|
| 2.3.1 Frames | 19 |
| 2.3.2 Media Access Control (MAC) | 20 |
| 2.4 Why Ethernet? | 22 |
| 2.4.1 Flexibility | 22 |
| 2.4.2 Large Installed Base | 24 |
| 2.4.3 Low Cost per Connection | 24 |
| 2.4.4 Reliability | 25 |
| 2.4.5 Scalability | 25 |
| 2.4.6 Summary of Why Ethernet | 25 |
| 2.5 Why Not Ethernet? | 26 |
| 2.6 Chapter Summary | 26 |
| 2.6.1 Major Concepts | 27 |
| 2.7 Chapter 2 Review Questions | 28 |

**Chapter 3: Ethernet Versions . . . . . . . . . . . . 29**

|  |  |
|---|---|
| 3.1 Ethernet Version 1 | 29 |
| 3.2 Common Ground | 30 |
| 3.2.1 Two Views—Architecture and Implementation | 30 |
| 3.2.2 Layering | 31 |
| 3.3 Ethernet Version 2 | 33 |
| 3.3.1 Collision Presence Signal and Collision Presence Test | 33 |

  3.3.2 Ethernet Version 2
  Frame Format .................. 33
  3.3.3 Preamble ................. 35
  3.3.4 Destination Address ......... 35
  3.3.5 Source Address ............ 36
  3.3.6 Type Field ............... 36
  3.3.7 Data Field ............... 36
  3.3.8 Frame Check Sequence (FCS) .. 36
 3.4 IEEE 802.3 Standard ............. 37
  3.4.1 Signal Quality Error (SQE) .... 37
  3.4.2 IEEE 802.3 Standard
  Frame Format .................. 37
  3.4.3 Preamble ................. 39
  3.4.4 Start Frame Delimiter (SFD) .. 39
  3.4.5 Destination Address ......... 39
  3.4.6 Source Address ............ 39
  3.4.7 Length Field / Type Field ..... 39
  3.4.8 Data Field ............... 40
  3.4.9 Frame Check Sequence ....... 40
 3.5 Chapter Summary ................ 40
 3.6 Major Concepts ................. 41
 3.7 Vocabulary .................... 42
 3.8 Chapter 3 Review Questions ........ 43

CONTENTS

**Chapter 4:** **10Mbps Ethernet** ............. **45**

    4.1 Introduction .................... 45
    4.2 Data Link Layer ................. 46
        4.2.1 Logical Link Control (LLC) .... 46
        4.2.2 Media Access Control (MAC) ... 47
        4.2.3 Physical Layer ............. 49
        4.2.4 Ethernet Physical
        Layer Building Blocks. ............ 50
        4.2.5 Physical Medium ............ 50
        4.2.6 Medium Dependent
        Interface (MDI) .................. 50
        4.2.7 Medium Attachment Unit (MAU) 51
        4.2.8 Attachment Unit Interface (AUI) 51
        4.2.9 Data Terminal Equipment (DTE) 51
        4.2.10 Building Blocks Summary .... 52
    4.3 Chapter Summary ................ 53
        4.3.1 Major Concepts ............. 53
    4.4 Vocabulary ...................... 54
    4.5 Chapter 4 Review Questions ........ 56

**Chapter 5:** **Fast Ethernet** ................. **57**

    5.1 Introduction .................... 57
    5.2 Modifications to the 802.3 Standard .. 58

## Contents

5.3 Clause 21—100BASE-T Introduction ... 59
    5.3.1 100BASE-T Clauses in Relation to the OSI Model ......... 59
    5.3.2 Common Information ......... 59
5.4 Clause 22—Media Independent Interface (MII) .................. 60
    5.4.1 Medium Independent Interface (MII) .................. 60
    5.4.2 Reconciliation Sublayer ....... 60
5.5 Clause 23—100BASE-T4 Transceiver ... 62
    5.5.1 Physical Details ............. 62
    5.5.2 Physical Coding Sublayer (PCS) . 64
5.6 Clause 24—100BASE-X Transceiver .. 64
5.7 Clause 25—TX PMD ............... 65
5.8 Clause 26—FX PMD ............... 65
5.9 Clause 27—Repeaters ............. 67
5.10 Clause 28—Auto-Negotiation ....... 67
5.11 Clause 29—Topology ............. 67
5.12 Clause 30—Management .......... 68
5.13 Summary ....................... 68
    5.13.1 Major Concepts ............ 69
5.14 Vocabulary ...................... 70
5.15 Chapter 5 Review Questions ....... 71

## CONTENTS

**Chapter 6:  100BASE-T2, T4, and TX . . . . . . .  73**

    6.1 Introduction . . . . . . . . . . . . . . . . . . . . .  73
    6.2 100BASE-T Media . . . . . . . . . . . . . . . . .  73
        6.2.1 Twisted Pair . . . . . . . . . . . . . . . .  74
        6.2.2 Shielded and Unshielded Cables . .  74
        6.2.3 Category 3 (CAT3) Cabling . . . .  75
        6.2.4 Category 5 (CAT5) Cabling . . . .  75
    6.3 100BASE-T2 . . . . . . . . . . . . . . . . . . . . .  75
        6.3.1 100BASE-T2 Media . . . . . . . . . .  75
    6.4 100BASE-T2 Pin Assignments . . . . . . .  78
    6.5 100BASE-T2 Crossover . . . . . . . . . . . .  78
        6.5.1 100BASE-T2 Repeaters . . . . . . .  79
        6.5.2 100BASE-T2 Link
        Integrity Check . . . . . . . . . . . . . . . . . .  80
    6.6 100BASE-T4 . . . . . . . . . . . . . . . . . . . . .  80
        6.6.1 100BASE-T4 Media . . . . . . . . . .  80
    6.7 100BASE-T4 Pin Assignments . . . . . . .  82
    6.8 100BASE-T4 Crossover . . . . . . . . . . . .  83
        6.8.1 100BASE-T4 Repeaters . . . . . . .  83
        6.8.2 100BASE-T4 Link
        Integrity Check . . . . . . . . . . . . . . . . . .  84
    6.9 100BASE-TX . . . . . . . . . . . . . . . . . . . . .  84
        6.9.1 100BASE-TX Media . . . . . . . . . .  85
    6.10 100BASE-TX Pin Assignments . . . . .  87
    6.11 100BASE-TX Crossover . . . . . . . . . . .  87
        6.11.1 100BASE-TX Repeaters . . . . . .  88

## Contents

|  |  |
|---|---|
| 6.11.2 100BASE-TX Link Integrity Check .................. | 88 |
| 6.12 Chapter 6 Review Questions ....... | 89 |

### Chapter 7: 100BASE-FX .................. 91

|  |  |
|---|---|
| 7.1 Introduction ..................... | 91 |
| 7.2 100BASE-FX .................... | 91 |
| 7.2.1 100BASE-FX Media .......... | 91 |
| 7.2.2 100BASE-FX Repeaters ....... | 92 |
| 7.2.3 100BASE-FX Link Integrity Check .................. | 93 |

### Chapter 8: Media ....................... 95

|  |  |
|---|---|
| 8.1 Introduction ..................... | 95 |
| 8.2 AUI ........................... | 95 |
| 8.3 Thick Coax (10BASE5) ............. | 98 |
| 8.4 Fiber Optic (10BASE-F, 100BASE-FX) .. | 100 |
| 8.5 Thin Coax (10BASE2) ............. | 101 |
| 8.6 Unshielded Twisted Pair (UTP) (IEEE 10BASE-T, 100BASE-TX, 100BASE-T2, 100BASE-T4) ......... | 103 |
| 8.7 Chapter Summary ................ | 105 |
| 8.7.1 Major Concepts ............ | 105 |
| 8.8 Chapter 8 Review Questions ........ | 106 |

ix

## CONTENTS

**Chapter 9: Hardware** .................... **107**

    9.1 Introduction ..................... 107
    9.2 Transceivers ..................... 108
    9.3 Repeaters ....................... 108
        9.3.1 10Mbps Ethernet Repeater Rules ................. 113
        9.3.2 Fast Ethernet Repeater Rules .. 114
        9.3.3 Class I Repeater ............ 114
        9.3.4 Class II Repeater ........... 115
        9.3.5 Repeater Summary .......... 115
    9.4 Bridges .......................... 115
    9.5 Switches ......................... 118
        9.5.1 Store-And-Forward .......... 119
        9.5.2 Cut-Through ............... 119
        9.5.3 Modified Cut-Through ........ 120
    9.6 Routers .......................... 120
    9.7 Network Interface Card (NIC) ....... 122
    9.8 Review Questions ................. 123

**Chapter 10: Design** ....................... **125**

    10.1 Introduction .................... 125
    10.2 Three Basic Rules ............... 126
        10.2.1 Keep It Simple ............ 127
        10.2.2 Document Everything ....... 129
        10.2.3 Staying within the Rules ..... 131

## Contents

- 10.3 Rules .......................... 132
  - 10.3.1 Lengths ................... 132
  - 10.3.2 Number of Nodes ........... 132
  - 10.3.3 Hardware Rules ............ 133
- 10.4 Design Step One ................ 133
  - 10.4.1 Automated Method of Estimating Network Requirements .. 135
  - 10.4.2 Manual Method of Estimating Network Requirements .. 135
- 10.5 Design Step Two ................ 137
  - 10.5.1 Quantifying the Traffic Information ..................... 137
- 10.6 Design Step Three .............. 139
- 10.7 Design Step Four ............... 140
- 10.8 Design Step Five ............... 141
- 10.9 Design Step Six ................ 144
  - 10.9.1 Optical Fiber .............. 144
  - 10.9.2 Twisted Pair ............... 144
  - 10.9.3 Thin Coax .................. 145
  - 10.9.4 Thick Coax ................. 145
- 10.10 Design Step Seven ............. 146
- 10.11 Design Step Eight ............. 148
  - 10.11.1 Selecting the Hardware .... 148
  - 10.11.2 Selecting a Manufacturer ... 149
- 10.12 The Final Step ................ 149
- 10.13 Chapter Summary ............... 150

## CONTENTS

        10.13.1 Major Concepts ........... 150
        10.14 Case Study .................... 152
        10.15 Review Questions .............. 158

**Chapter 11: Installation ................... 159**

        11.1 Introduction .................... 159
        11.2 The Decision to Contract .......... 160
            11.2.1 Scope of Project ........... 160
            11.2.2 Size and Qualifications
                 of Labor Pool .................. 162
            11.2.3 The Final Decision .......... 163
        11.3 Selecting a Contractor ........... 163
            11.3.1 Where to Look for a Contractor . 165
            11.3.2 How to Interview a Contractor .. 165
            11.3.3 Making the Final Decision .... 166
        11.4 The First Step .................. 167
        11.5 What to Watch For .............. 168
        11.6 Documentation .................. 169
            11.6.1 Notes ..................... 169
            11.6.2 Drawings .................. 169
            11.6.3 Measurements .............. 170
        11.7 Getting Ready .................. 170
            11.7.1 Getting Ready Step 1 ........ 171
            11.7.2 Getting Ready Step 2 ........ 171
            11.7.3 Getting Ready Step 3 ........ 171

## Contents

                11.8 Starting the Installation .......... 174
                      11.8.1 Installation—Step One ...... 174
                      11.8.2 Installation—Step Two ...... 175
                      11.8.3 Installation—Step Three ..... 176
                      11.8.4 Installation—Step Four ...... 176
                      11.8.5 Installation—Step Five ...... 177
                      Getting Started—
                      Installation Step Six .............. 177
                11.9 Case Study ..................... 178
                11.10 Chapter 11 Review Questions ..... 182

**Chapter 12: Maintenance** .................. **183**

                12.1 Introduction .................... 183
                12.2 Connectivity Maintenance ......... 184
                      12.2.1 The VOM ................ 184
                      12.2.2 The TDR ................. 185
                      12.2.3 The Hand-Held Cable Tester ... 185
                      12.2.4 Connectivity Preventative
                      Maintenance .................... 187
                      12.2.5 Connectivity Corrective
                      Maintenance .................... 188
                12.3 Equipment Maintenance .......... 188
                      12.3.1 Equipment Preventative
                      Maintenance .................... 188
                      12.3.2 Equipment Corrective
                      Maintenance .................... 189

## CONTENTS

12.4 Network Management ............ 189
    12.4.1 Using Special Equipment
    and/or Software ................ 190
    12.4.2 The Manual Method ....... 192
    12.4.3 Getting Started with
    Corrective Maintenance .......... 193
12.5 Case Study ..................... 193
12.6 Chapter Summary ............... 197
12.7 Chapter 12 Review Questions ...... 198

## Chapter 13: The Future of Ethernet ........ 199

13.1 Introduction ................... 199
    13.1.1 Data Types and Sizes ....... 200
    13.1.2 Network Traffic Implications .. 201
    13.1.3 Networking Requirements .... 201
13.2 Strategy for Survival ............. 202
    13.2.1 Migration ................ 202
    13.2.2 Scalability ............... 203
    13.2.3 Cost of Ownership ......... 203
    13.2.4 Flexibility ................ 204
13.3 Gigabit Ethernet Technology
Overview ........................ 204
13.4 Gigabit Migration ................ 205
13.5 Conclusion ..................... 206
13.6 Chapter Summary ............... 207
    13.6.1 Major Concepts ........... 207

## Contents

**Appendix A: Collision Domain Basics** ....... **209**

**Appendix B: EIA/TIA Cable Categories** ...... **211**

    B.1 Common Specifications ............ 211
        B.1.1 General .................. 212
    B.2 Category 3 ....................... 212
    B.3 Category 4 ....................... 213
    B.4 Category 5 ....................... 213

**Appendix C: Twisted-Pair Wiring Diagrams** .................... **215**

    C.1 10BASE-T, 100BASE-TX, and 100BASE-T2 Pin Assignments ...... 216
    C.2 10BASE-T, 100BASE-TX, and 100BASE-T2 Crossover ............ 217
    C.3 100BASE-T4 Pin Assignments ...... 217
    C.4 100BASE-T4 Crossover ............ 218

**Appendix D: Abbreviations and Acronyms** ... **219**

**Appendix E: Other Sources of Information** ... **235**

**Glossary** .................................. **237**

**Index** ..................................... **245**

xv

# Preface

When I started working with computer systems over 18 years ago, memory was core and 32KB was considered a luxury. Networks were in the formative stages. Documentation was scarce and what could be found was usually written by an engineer for readers with technical backgrounds.

A few years have passed; memory is now semiconductor and 32MB is not considered unusual. Networks can be found in practically every company with a few PCs, but good books for the novice are still hard to find. There are many sources from which to choose, but few deliver the information that is really needed.

My first experiences with data communications were with Digital Equipment Corporation (DEC) VT50 terminals and Teletype hard-copy terminals. Communications to these terminals required close proximity to the host computer, a separate line to each terminal, and a dedicated Input/Output (I/O) control port for each. The terminals were called "dumb" because they could only display and transmit characters with no other processing capabilities. The cost for "dumb" terminals in the '70s rivals what we would pay today for a well-equipped Personal Computer (PC).

I consider it a great honor to have been in the industry long enough to experience such significant changes. In an industry characterized by these changes, it is noteworthy when there is a standard or technology that is crafted carefully enough to still be a cornerstone after 14 years. Ethernet is such a technology. Since the release of version 2 in November of 1982, it has become, and remains, the dominant Local Area Network (LAN) technology.

This book is written to accomplish three purposes:

1. An introduction to Local Area Networking, which will provide the basic understanding of LANs, including relative history and concepts.
2. An introduction to Ethernet, what it is, what the versions are, and a technical overview of how it functions.
3. A brief tutorial on the basic concepts of design, installation, and maintenance of a simple Ethernet network, complete with case studies.

This book is targeted for the networking novice interested in the fundamentals of Ethernet and of the design, installation, or troubleshooting of a simple Ethernet network. It contains information to help you really get started. Basic information is provided about technical aspects of Ethernet and Fast Ethernet, their standards, cable types and rules, and hardware and rules. A case study at the end of the chapters on design, installation, and maintenance illustrates the theories presented and shows how to put them into practice.

I have expanded and rewritten this book considerably from the previous two versions. This expansion and rewriting are a direct result of feedback from readers and from watching the threads in the comp.dcom.lans.ethernet newsgroup.

## Preface

This book is organized into thirteen chapters and five appendices.

- Chapter 1 is an introduction to local area networking.
- Chapter 2 is an introduction to Ethernet. It provides a brief history of Ethernet and discusses the core of what Ethernet is.
- Chapter 3 discusses Ethernet versions. This chapter covers Ethernet versions 1 and 2, and the IEEE 802.3 standard. Common properties, details of operation, and differences are covered in this chapter.
- Chapter 4 is a discussion of 10Mbps Ethernet.
- Chapter 5 is a discussion of 100Mbps Ethernet or Fast Ethernet.
- Chapter 6 provides an overview of 100BASE-T technologies.
- Chapter 7 presents an overview of 100BASE-FX
- Chapter 8 covers the basic media types for Ethernet and Fast Ethernet.
- Chapter 9 is about the hardware that is used in Ethernet networks.
- Chapter 10 discusses the basics of network design.
- Chapter 11 covers the basics of network installation.
- Chapter 12 covers the basics of network maintenance.
- Chapter 13 is a discussion of the future of Ethernet.
- Appendix A covers some collision domain basics.
- Appendix B is the EIA/TIA cabling specifications.
- Appendix C contains wiring diagrams for the basic UTP cables.
- Appendix D is an acronym guide that covers not only the acronyms in this book but many other networking and computer-related acronyms that you should find useful.
- Appendix E contains contact information for standards organizations.

# Acknowledgments

I would like to express my sincere gratitude to Richard Seifert for providing the review of this book. His work with the original Ethernet specifications and the IEEE 802.3 subcommittee over the years, as well as his years as an educator and consultant in the network and communications industry, provided tremendous insight and clarity to this work. I somehow managed to survive his red pen and am much better (certainly much better informed) for the experience.

I also would like to acknowledge the patience of my family. Without the support of my wife, daughter, and son, I would not have been able to complete this book.

# Chapter 1

# An Introduction to Local Area Networking

## 1.1 Local Area Networks

Local Area Networks, or LANs, are as common, and as taken for granted, as coffee pots in today's corporate environment. Most employees today have at least one computer system on their desk, whether for business, engineering, or other applications, that is connected to various other computer systems, specialized test equipment, printers, or file or database servers. This connectivity, the glue that provides cohesion to our workplace, within the local office or building, is provided by some sort of Local Area Network or LAN.

CHAPTER 1　　　　　　　　　An Introduction to Local Area Networking

The term network is defined by Webster's dictionary as "any arrangement of fabric or parallel wires, threads, etc. crossed at regular intervals by others."[1] If you have ever seen a wiring closet or worked with patch panels, it is easy to see the application of this definition.

## 1.2 Brief History

Over the years networking has evolved from the simple connection of terminals to mainframes and minicomputers, where all of the communications intelligence was in the host computer and the terminals were simply display and input devices, to the LANs of today. Now, LANs permit the well-defined attachment of computing resources such as printers, test equipment, sampling devices, and other computers to a common network. These network devices, often referred to as nodes, all contain a significant amount of communications intelligence.

The distribution of the communication control to the network devices allow for the decentralization of the computing environment. This decentralization permits computer resource and load sharing across multiple resources in an office setting or across the world.

---

[1] *Webster's Dictionary of the English Language*, Unabridged Vol. II (Chicago: J.G. Ferguson Publishing, 1977) p. 1207.

## 1.2.1 Serial Communications

Terminals that connected the user interface to mainframe and minicomputers were attached with a network of serial communications lines. There were two main methods of transmitting serial data: varying the current or varying the voltage.

When varying the current for signaling, the most common method was the 20 milliampere (20mA) current loop, which was originally used with teletype equipment. The liabilities of inability to support semi-intelligent devices, such as modems, and the often high voltage requirements for operation led the way to the voltage varying techniques for the transmission of serial data.

The most common method for transmitting data by varying voltage was the Electronic Industry Association (EIA) RS-232 standard. This method transmitted data in a binary fashion by producing a positive voltage to represent a binary 0 and a negative voltage to represent a binary 1.

Both of these methods required communications hardware resident on the host computer. This I/O controller provided the control to receive data from the bus, place it in the proper serial format, and transmit it to the terminal. Data transmitted from the terminal was received by the I/O controller, which interrupted the processor so that the data could be received and processed.

## 1.2.2 More Advanced Terminals and Connectivity

International Business Machines (IBM) broke the traditional model of using point-to-point serial communications connections to terminal equipment in 1974 with the introduction of a series of terminals that used a loop of coaxial cable to connect a group of terminals back to the main computer.

In this method, the I/O controller transmitted data to the terminals one at a time in a sequential fashion. The IBM terminals were able to store up keystroke information and would transmit the data to the host computer when the I/O controller made the request during the polling cycle.

Soon there were several companies researching a variety of technologies for providing local area communications for computer resources. In 1977, Datapoint Corporation started marketing the Attached Resource Computer Network, also known as ARCNET.

The main difference of the new LAN technologies being developed was the inclusion of intelligent control at the network resource end. Datapoint's ARCNET was the beginning of a LAN technology explosion that continues to this day with no end in sight.

## 1.2.3 Topologies

The term topology can be confusing as it can be used to refer to the logical or physical layout of a LAN.

### Logical Topology

Most commonly, topology refers to the logical representation of the interconnection of network devices. This is how the LAN is most commonly perceived and it provides a useful model for conceptualizing. The description of the LAN, both in word and drawing, will reflect the logical operation of the LAN instead of the actual physical implementation of the electrical components.

### Physical Topology

The physical topology of the LAN is the geographical layout of the actual electrical circuit created. The physical structure, or implementation, of the LAN may take a different geographical layout than the logical topology.

### Common Topologies

Four of the most commonly used LAN topologies are logically described as ring, bus, star, and tree.

## 1.2.4 Ring

In this method, the data is passed from device to device on the ring until it arrives at its intended destination. There are multiple implementations of methods using single and multiple rings for transferring

CHAPTER 1 An Introduction to Local Area Networking

data, permitting a single packet or multiple packets to be placed on the ring simultaneously. The physical implementation of this method is often a star.

## 1.2.5 Bus

The typical bus topology utilizes a coaxial cable to connect multiple computer resources to each other. Speeds, media, and signaling methods vary widely depending on implementation.

The most popular bus topology is the 10BASE2 LAN implementation, discussed in detail later in this book. This implementation uses coaxial cables to connect with tee connectors in the back of the attached network resources (see Fig. 1.1).

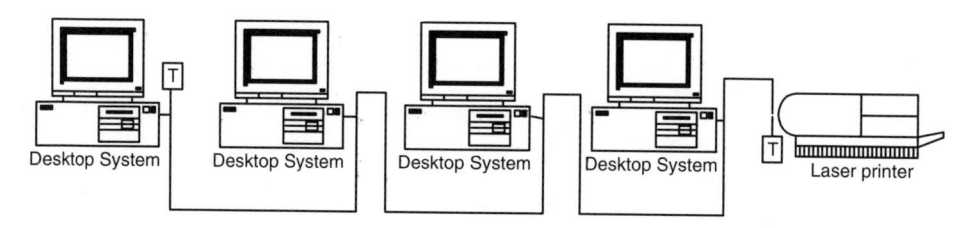

**Figure 1.1:** 10BASE2 bus topology

One very popular bus topology was, and still is, the Hewlett Packard Interface Bus (HP-IB) implementation. While it is not a LAN, it provides a clear view of this topology. This implementation, introduced in 1965 and now the IEEE 488 standard, uses cables connected from system to system (or device to device) in a daisy chain configuration: eight data lines, which carry data and command messages; three control, or handshake lines, which manage the control of data exchange between connected devices; and five interface management lines used to manage the interfaces on the attached devices (see Fig. 1.2).

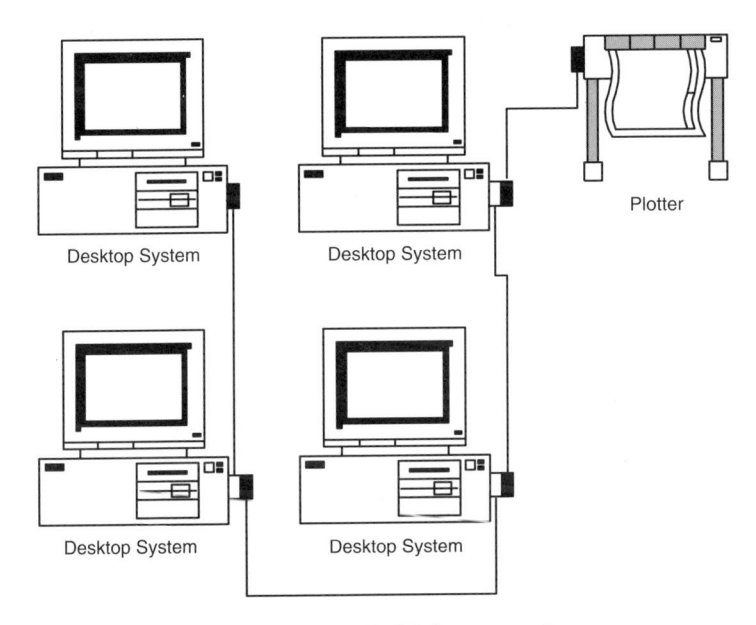

**Figure 1.2:** HP-IB bus topology

## 1.2.6 Star

Star topology is sometimes referred to as a hub topology. In this arrangement, all of the network devices are directly connected to a common network device like a hub or controller. Communication from any network device to another passes through this central network device (see Fig. 1.3).

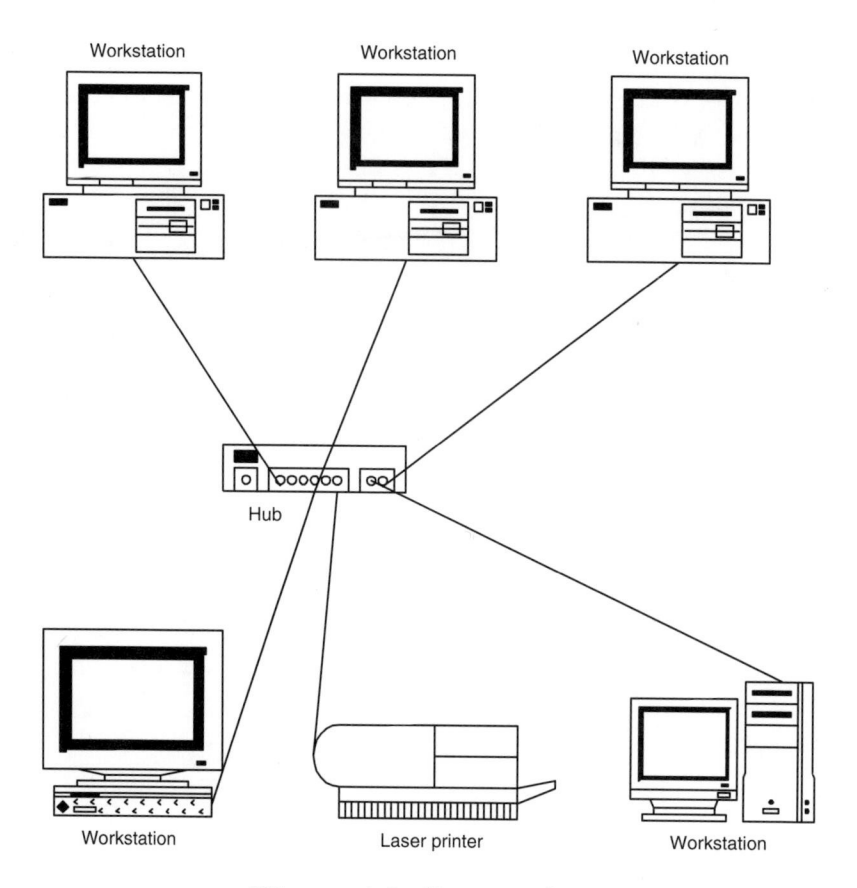

**Figure 1.3:** Star topology

## 1.2.7 Tree

The *root* or top of the tree structure is the point from which other extended bus segments radiate out toward the network devices. From

## 1.2 Brief History

some of these network devices other network segments may radiate downward to provide network connectivity to other network devices. The best example of this structure is where a network hub is the root and segments radiate from the headend to network devices such as computers and printers while also radiating to other hubs. These hubs in turn radiate down to other network devices, possibly including other hubs (see Fig. 1.4).

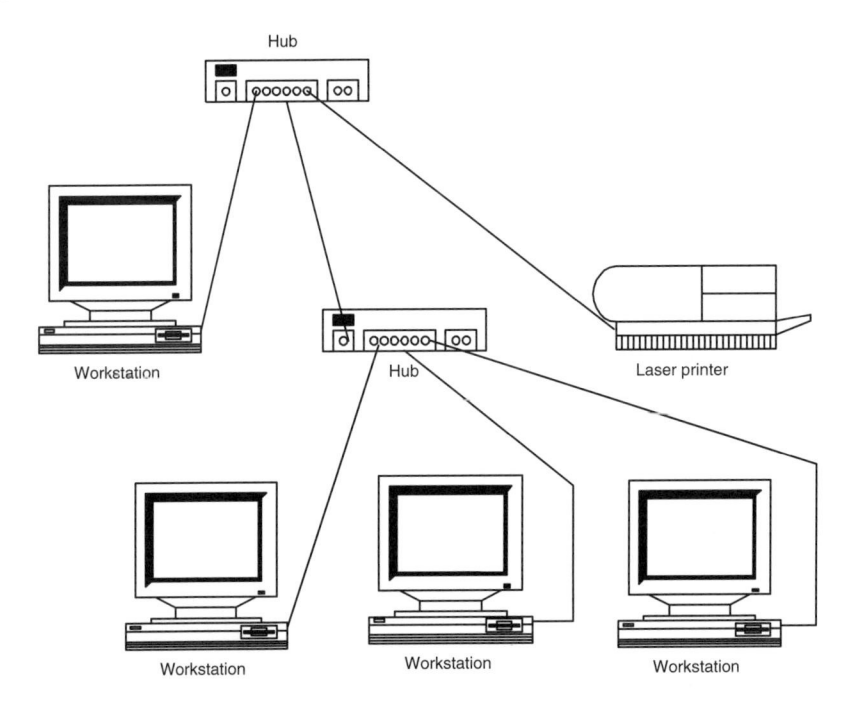

**Figure 1.4:** Tree topology

CHAPTER 1 _An Introduction to Local Area Networking_

## 1.2.8 Topology Summary

Many networks use a mixture of topologies to accomplish their final design. The most common example of combining topologies is the use of network hubs to service isolated office areas and the interconnection of those hubs. This combination ultimately results in a star and bus topology.

# 1.3 LAN/WAN

It is important to understand the distinction between local area networking and wide area networking. The importance is based on the available technologies for the transmission of data across local and wide areas.

LANs are typically constrained to a single building or building complex. They are characterized by high data transfer rates, typically 10Mbps or greater (soon to be 1 gigabit per second), and low error rates.

Wide Area Networks (WANs) are typically used to interconnect geographically separate areas. These areas may be a block apart or on separate continents. They are characterized by lower data transmission rates, typically 56Kbps to 1.544Mbps (although data rates of up to 155Mbps are available), and higher error rates.

## 1.4 ISO/OSI

In any discussion of networking, some coverage of the International Organization for Standardization(ISO) Open Systems Interconnect (OSI) model is appropriate. This model is important because it aids in conceptualizing the networking process in a modular form. With this model, each separate aspect of the networking process is broken down into one of seven layers. Each of the layers deals with a separate functional part of the networking process. Ethernet is best represented by the lower two layers of the OSI model.

The ISO developed the OSI networking model with the goal of describing a common, open method of connecting computer systems together to exchange information. The OSI is not a network, but a model that networks can be described with. It is important to note that the OSI model is a concept and that each of the layers is not necessarily represented by a single physical device or software (or firmware) module. In the real world of functioning commercial products, it is common for any given hardware device or software (or firmware) module to cross the boundaries set by this model.

The layers of the OSI model are stacked on top of one another with layer one at the bottom working up to layer seven at the top. Each layer of the model is independent of the others and has well-defined methods for the transference of data between the layers. As data travels up and down the structure of the model, information is added and

CHAPTER 1 *An Introduction to Local Area Networking*

removed from the headers and data changes from user recognizable formats, such as spreadsheets (above layer seven), to computer recognizable binary data (at layer one). At each layer, functionality is added or removed as required. Table 1.1 provides a quick, functional overview of the OSI model.

**Table 1.1:** A Function Overview of the OSI Model

| Layer | Name | Function |
|---|---|---|
| 7 | Application Layer | Interface for applications. Provides standard formats for applications to send and receive data through the functions and services of lower layers. |
| 6 | Presentation Layer | Formatting of data from lower layers so that it can be understood by an application. Also responsible for the formatting of Layer 7 data to be passed down to lower layers. |
| 5 | Session Layer | Controls the connection and disconnection of the data communications path or session and determines the rules for communications. |
| 4 | Transport Layer | Provides connection reliability through the networks required to pass the data. |
| 3 | Networks Layer | Establishes the path that the data will traverse through the network. Data at this layer is contained in what is termed as a packet. |
| 2 | Data Link Layer | Provides the mechanisms to activate, maintain, and deactivate the link. This layer also provides error detection and, in connection-oriented links, control essential for the higher layers to reliably exchange data. |
| 1 | Physical Layer | Provides the electrical, mechanical, control functions, and procedural specifications for the activation, maintenance, and deactivation of the physical link between systems. |

*1.5 Chapter Summary*

The OSI model is a description of a method to modularize networking. Real applications of network implementation do not need to meet the ideals of this model. In real applications, all of the layers are not necessarily implemented. The OSI model also provides for independence of the layers while, in practice, the intended independence between the layers is not always achieved.

Ethernet is one implementation of the first two layers of the OSI model.

# 1.5 Chapter Summary

The history of local area networking helps us to understand how we arrived at our current technologies. It also assists us in putting into perspective our current technological position.

## 1.5.1 Major Concepts

An important concept of serial communications and the early IBM loop communications is that the I/O control was completely placed within the host computer. The attached terminals were not intelligent, that is, they did not have the processing power to perform any error checking or communication control.

The lack of intelligence on the terminals is also important to note. In the serial communications environment, the terminals required one I/O control port each. Each port controlled the input and output

CHAPTER 1 　　　　　　　　　An Introduction to Local Area Networking

of data to and from the terminal. This put the onus on the I/O controller to manage all communication to the single terminal device. In the IBM loop scenario, the I/O controller had more responsibility in that it had to manage multiple terminal interaction.

It is important to note that during those years the marketplace was such that each vendor was in the mode of producing proprietary systems and devices with closed architectures. There was a significant shift in this thinking as vendors started to respond to the marketplace demands for a more open computing environment (the early 1980s). As LAN technology developed, more intelligence was given to the individual network devices.

In our discussion of LANs and WANs, it is important to note the geographical and data transfer rate differences.

In the overview of the ISO/OSI model, the concept of layers is the main point to understand. It is also important to understand that the model is simply a description, and that real applications often vary from this ideal.

## 1.6 Vocabulary

### LAN

Local Area Network. Typically constrained to a single building or building complex. LANs are characterized by high data transfer rates, typically 10Mbps or greater (soon to be 1 gigabit per second), and lower error rates.

## Network

The fabric of media that connects computing resources to facilitate the exchange of data.

## Topology

The logical representation of the interconnection of network devices.

## WAN

Wide Area Network. Typically used to interconnect geographically separate areas. These areas may be a block apart or on separate continents. WANs are characterized by lower data transmission rates, typically 56Kbps to 1.544Mbps, and higher error rates.

# 1.7 Chapter 1 Review Questions

1. What is significantly different between serial communications and a LAN?

2. What are two of the differences between a LAN and a WAN?

3. Briefly describe the ring topology.

4. Briefly describe the bus topology.

*CHAPTER 1*  *An Introduction to Local Area Networking*

5. Briefly describe the star topology.

6. Briefly describe the tree topology.

7. What is the headend or root?

# Chapter 2

# Introduction to Ethernet

## 2.1 Introduction

Many different types of networks have been used to connect computer systems. The most common networks include Ethernet, Token Ring, FDDI, and ATM. Each network type comes with its own package of advantages and liabilities. Some provide high-speed transmission with a relatively high cost per connection, while others provide low-cost connections with slower transmission speeds. Some are designed to handle file type data, others are designed to handle voice or video, and some are designed to carry multiple types of data. Another area of difference is that each network has a different type of test equipment, requiring varying budgets to purchase, as well as varying levels of expertise to operate. Finally, some networking solutions are common across multiple computer systems' platforms—from PCs to high-end workstations.

CHAPTER 2                                              Introduction to Ethernet

## 2.2 A Brief History

The original design of Ethernet is attributed to Dr. Robert Metcalfe and David Boggs, who in 1973 ran the first LAN for personal computers, called the ALTO systems, which were manufactured by Xerox. This first LAN was referred to as "experimental Ethernet." This name was used to refer to the experimental network while it was under development. Once it was operational, Metcalfe renamed it Ethernet after the "luminiferous ether through which electromagnetic radiation was once thought to propagate."[2] This network ran at 2.94Mbps (clocked from the ALTO system clock with a steady pulse every 340 nanoseconds).

Digital, Intel, and Xerox started working together in late 1979 on standardizing Ethernet technology. The result was the publication of "The Ethernet, A Local Area Network: Data Link Layer and Physical Layer Specifications, Version 1.0." This consortium of three—Digital, Intel, and Xerox—became known as DIX.

The three companies continued to work together on the refinement of the Ethernet specification and in 1982 published "The Ethernet, A Local Area Network: Data Link Layer and Physical Layer Specifications, Version 2.0."

The Institute of Electrical and Electronic Engineers (IEEE) formed a committee for the promotion of LAN standards called Project 802. The IEEE 802.3 subcommittee was formed in 1982 to create an international standard based on DIX specifications.

---

[2] Robert Breyer and Sean Riley, *Switched and Fast Ethernet* (California: Ziff-Davis Press, 1995) p. 3.

## 2.3 What Is Ethernet?

Ethernet is the most popular LAN technology, representing over 80 percent of installed network connections.

The IEEE 802.3 standard is based on the Ethernet version 2 standard. In this book the term Ethernet will be used to refer to both the Ethernet version 2.0 standards and the IEEE 802.3 specifications, as the two have become synonymous. All Ethernet equipment manufactured since 1985 conforms, or attempts to conform, to the IEEE 802.3 standard.

The Ethernet version 2 specification is not an active standard like the IEEE 802.3 specifications. This simply means that there are committees that have the charter to upgrade the 802.3 specifications on a regular basis.

There are three elements that comprise Ethernet. The first is the frame that the data is packed into for transmission. The second element is a set of rules for access arbitration called the Media Access Control (MAC). The MAC is based on a concept called Carrier Sense Multiple Access with Collision Detection (CSMA/CD). The third component of Ethernet is the physical medium on which the signals are carried.

### 2.3.1 Frames

Ethernet packages data into frames for transmission. The frame is a well-defined structure containing information about the sender, the intended receiver, the type or length of frame, actual data, and a Cyclic Redundancy Check (CRC). The Ethernet version 2 and IEEE 802.3 standard frames are covered in more detail in Chapter 3.

## 2.3.2 Media Access Control (MAC)

The Media Access Control (MAC) is a set of rules that control access to the network for the transmission of data. The MAC is one of the main differentiating factors of networking types. Ethernet MAC is contention based.

When an Ethernet node is ready to transmit a frame, it listens for or attempts to *sense* traffic on the network. The traffic that the node is listening for is made up of signals that carry the transmitted information, which are called *carriers*. The term carrier is a throwback to radio terminology; a better term may be activity. When traffic is detected, the node waits until the traffic clears (deferring). If the node does not sense a carrier, or activity, then it proceeds to transmit. This process, of listening for the activity before transmission, is called carrier sense.

It is not enough that the node that is ready to transmit a frame waits for the network to be quiet before transmitting. The receiving nodes are given a set time, called the interpacket gap time, to determine that the previous packet has ended and to prepare to receive the next packet.

As multiple devices are permitted to attach to the LAN, the network is therefore said to be *multiple access*. Due to the fact that Ethernet is multiple access, there is a possibility of two or more nodes transmitting at the same time.

When two nodes transmit simultaneously, a *collision* occurs on the network. The network hardware is equipped to detect the collisions by a process called *collision detection*. The term collision is another unfortunate choice of words. A more appropriate choice might be arbitration

## 2.3 What Is Ethernet?

cycle.[3] When a collision occurs, each of the transmitting nodes will continue to transmit for a brief period of time in order to assure that the collision is propagated throughout the entire network, a *jam signal*. This is done so that all the transmitters are made aware of the collision. After the transmission of the jam signal is complete, each of the transmitting nodes involved in the collision will wait a random period of time and then attempt to retransmit the frames.

If a node that is retransmitting because of a previous collision detects that the transmission has been involved in another collision, the medium is known to be busy. The node will attempt to adjust the load on the medium by *backing off*. The process of backoff is to take the previous wait time, generated at the first collision, and double it before continuing with the normal transmission of the message. If the message is involved in another collision, then this backoff process is repeated, doubling the random numbers for the wait time for each occurrence, until the message has been involved with ten collisions. From the tenth to the sixteenth collision the wait time is generated from the random number pool made available in the tenth collision. When the message has reached the maximum number of collisions, sixteen, the controller will cease attempting to transmit and will generate an error message.

This method of transmission is called Carrier Sense Multiple Access with Collision Detection or CSMA/CD, which is what Ethernet and the IEEE 802.3 standard are. Based on reflections from Rich Seifert (one of the original authors of Ethernet versions 1 and 2, and

---

[3] From an interview with Rich Seifert.

CHAPTER 2                                     *Introduction to Ethernet*

a major contributor to the IEEE 802.3 specifications), a better phrase may be activity sense multiple access with arbitration methodology. As described in the previous paragraphs, Ethernet and the IEEE 802.3 standard allow multiple systems to access the network using a carrier sensing technique. Should a collision occur, the network is capable of detecting and recovering from the collision (see Fig. 2.1).

## 2.4 Why Ethernet?

The major benefits of the Ethernet are its flexibility, large installed base, low cost per connection, reliability, and scalability.

### 2.4.1 Flexibility

Ethernet can be implemented across multiple platforms and is easily expanded. Almost every major computer manufacturer provides an Ethernet connection to their workstations and PCs, either as standard equipment or as an option. Some PC systems require a Network Interface Card (NIC), but these are generally inexpensive. The availability of a common connection on a broad array of dissimilar systems allows these systems to be attached to a single LAN.

With the network being the same between dissimilar systems, software connectivity tools (or protocols) will be required at layers three and above to provide file transfer and other services, such as remote login. These connectivity tools are also common, inexpensive, and simple to find.

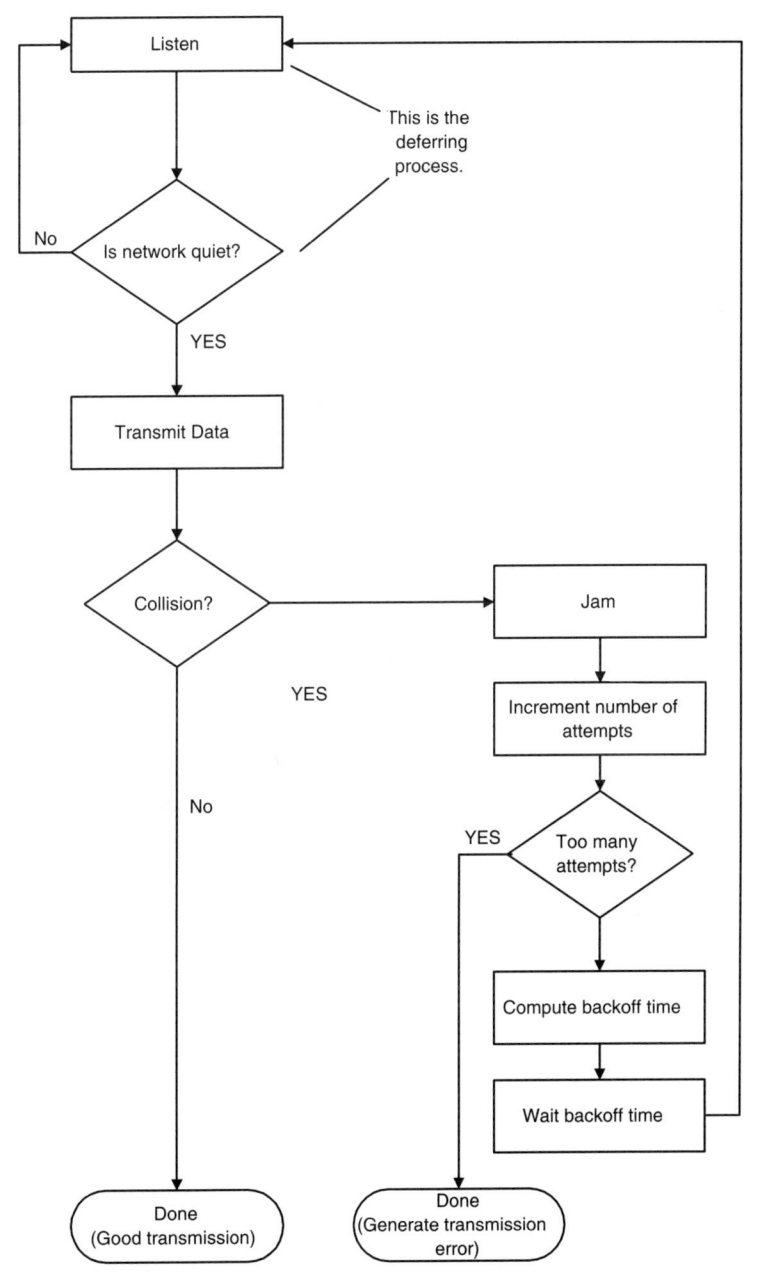

**Figure 2.1:** Simplified transmit diagram

## 2.4.2 Large Installed Base

Ethernet has proven to be a stable networking base for over a decade, and many manufacturers provide Ethernet connections on their systems. The popularity of Ethernet has resulted in a large installed base of systems interconnected using this technology.

The user base continues to grow as companies with 10Mbps Ethernet upgrade to 100Mbs Ethernet and continue to invest in Ethernet technology.

The already enormous installed base and the continuing growth of the Ethernet market continue to promote new product development and ensure support for existing equipment.

## 2.4.3 Low Cost per Connection

Ethernet has been implemented on several types of media, which will be discussed in greater detail in Chapter 6. The equipment for the implementation of the network—hubs, switches, and network interface cards—are relatively inexpensive as well. This equipment is discussed in greater detail in Chapter 7.

Studies clearly show the decline in component cost of Ethernet networks. A 1996 Instat survey showed an expected 7 percent decline in the per port costs for hubs from 1996 to 1998. The same survey shows an expected 27 percent decline in the per port costs of hubs for Fast Ethernet for the same period. A 1996 study performed by IDC shows an estimated cost decrease of 72 percent for Ethernet and 27 percent for Fast Ethernet network interface cards from 1996 to 1998.

## 2.4.4 Reliability

Reliable networks are critical to the operation of today's companies. The longevity of Ethernet and the continuing evolution of its hardware technology have resulted in stability and reliability for everyone who uses the Ethernet.

## 2.4.5 Scalability

Ethernet version 2 was released in 1982, the 10Mbps IEEE 802.3 standards were released in 1985, 100Mbps (Fast Ethernet) specifications were released by the IEEE in 1995, and 1Gbps specifications are currently in the planning stages. The scalability of Ethernet is clear, as is its solid position for the future.

## 2.4.6 Summary of Why Ethernet

In general, Ethernet is an excellent solution for the connection of diverse collections of computer systems and other devices, such as printers and lab equipment, on a LAN. Ethernet provides a balance of cost, performance, and flexibility that matches most companies' LAN requirements.

The wide variety of protocols for use with Network Operating Systems (NOS), such as Novell's IPX protocol and the TCP/IP protocol suite, that are designed to run on Ethernet LANs show strong support from major manufacturers. The abundance of Ethernet connectivity built into major manufacturers' computer systems and equipment, such as Hewlett-Packard 32-bit workstations, also demonstrate strong industry support for Ethernet standards.

Ethernet has transmission rates of 10Mbps and 100Mbps, which are more than suitable for most business, engineering, medical, scientific, and other applications. While these transmission rates are satisfactory to many users, there are now manufacturers and consortiums investigating 1Gb/s Ethernet standards.

The long life and continuing improvements in the standards, equipment, and support are the ingredients for a stable, growth-minded, supportable network infrastructure.

Before running off to the Ethernet Camelot of networking, it would be prudent to ask why not Ethernet.

## 2.5 Why Not Ethernet?

The main reason why one would not consider Ethernet is that Ethernet is a local area networking topology and is not a solution for wide area networking requirements. Ethernet is suitable for providing networking capability for an office, building, or campus with its flexible topology.

## 2.6 Chapter Summary

In this chapter, a brief history and the fundamentals of Ethernet have been discussed. The history is important because it shows a steady progression of the standard. We have also discussed how it is important

*2.6 Chapter Summary*

because of how the consortium formed to standardize the Ethernet technology promoted it in such a way as to have it converted into an international standard and, by doing so, insured the longevity of the technology.

## 2.6.1 Major Concepts

Data transmitted in an Ethernet network is organized into well-defined frames that contain information about the sender and intended receiver, the type or length of a frame, actual data, and a CRC.

Ethernet version 2.0 and the IEEE 802.3 specifications are both based on the MAC concept of Carrier Sense Multiple Access with Collision Detection (CSMA/CD). Broken down into parts, this is where

- *Carrier Sense* refers to the fact the each network node listens to the network for traffic before attempting to transmit.
- *Multiple Access* refers to the ability for multiple systems to access the network simultaneously.
- *Collision Detection* refers to the ability for each node to detect that a collision has occurred and recover from the collision in a well-defined manner.

It is important to understand that collisions are not necessarily bad; they are part of the normal arbitration cycle for an Ethernet.

The Ethernet has three major benefits: flexibility, large installed base, and low cost per connection. These three benefits clearly demonstrate the stability of the technology and the market position of Ethernet technology.

## 2.7 Chapter 2 Review Questions

1. What are the three elements that comprise Ethernet?

2. Define MAC.

3. Define CSMA/CD.

4. What is a jam signal?

5. What are three major benefits of Ethernet?

6. What is the significance of each of the three major benefits of Ethernet?

7. When would one not select Ethernet for a networking technology?

# Chapter 3

# Ethernet Versions

There are three standards regarding Ethernet that you should have some basic understanding about. These standards are

- Ethernet version 1
- Ethernet version 2
- IEEE 802.3 standard

In this chapter there will be a very brief discussion of Ethernet version 1, followed by Ethernet version 2, and lastly the IEEE 802.3 standard. We will finish this chapter by showing the significant differences between Ethernet version 2 and the IEEE 802.3 standard.

## 3.1 Ethernet Version 1

There are two relevant facts that are important for you to know about Ethernet version 1. The first is that Ethernet version 1 is obsolete.

Therefore, if you are designing a new Ethernet network you will not need to worry about Ethernet version 1. The second is that Ethernet version 1 was never implemented by any major manufacturer. Given these two facts, there will be no more discussion of Ethernet version 1.

Ethernet version 1 was replaced with Ethernet version 2. The Ethernet version 2 standard was adopted and modified by the IEEE to become their 802.3 standard.

## 3.2 Common Ground

Before beginning the individual discussions of Ethernet version 2 and the IEEE 802.3 specifications, some of the common ground that these specifications share will be explored. The foundations of the IEEE 802.3 specification were founded in the Ethernet version 2 specifications. Both specifications are viewed from a logical perspective and use the concept of layering.

### 3.2.1 Two Views—Architecture and Implementation

Ethernet can be viewed from two main perspectives—architecture or implementation. The architecture is a logical view, while implementation is a physical view.

## 3.2 Common Ground

Architecture is defined as "emphasizing the logical divisions of the system, and how they fit together."[4]

Implementation, on the other hand, is defined as "emphasizing the actual components, their packaging and interconnection."[5]

This chapter is written from an architectural perspective, just as the specifications for both Ethernet version 2 and the IEEE 802.3 are. This view of the system allows the segmenting of Ethernet into smaller logical pieces. This provides the ability to see the structure of Ethernet with greater clarity.

It is important to remember that, while the architectural view provides clarity of presentation, the implementation view is concerned with the real product. This results in a lack of clear distinction of the boundaries between layers in actual implementation, which the architectural view makes so clear.

### 3.2.2 Layering

Ethernet deals with the bottom two layers of the OSI model. From the perspective of Ethernet there are three layers—the client, data link, and physical.

---

[4] Digital, Intel, and Xerox, The Ethernet, A Local Area Network, Data Link Layer and Physical Layer Specifications. Version 2, 1982.

[5] Ibid.

## Client Layer

The client layer is considered to be all layers collectively above Layer 2 of the OSI model. This collective view is formed because the identity and function(s) of higher level layers are irrelevant in this discussion of Ethernet, except in a general sense.

## Data Link Layer

The Data Link Layer defines the communications that are not dependent on the physical attachment to the transmission medium. This layer is located below the client layer and above the physical layer. The data link layer is responsible for connectionless point-to-point communications.

The primary purpose of the data link layer is to provide a mechanism to manage the link to the physical layer of the network, and the encapsulation and decapsulation of data going to and from the client layer.

Managing the link to the physical layer takes into consideration the major function of placing data on and retrieving data from the network. This function is concerned with the contention scheme for managing data flow. This contention scheme is covered in greater detail later in this book.

## Physical Layer

The physical layer provides electrical and physical connectivity. This layer defines the Medium Dependent Interface (MDI), which is simply the cable connections and how the data is encoded onto the physical medium.

## 3.3 Ethernet Version 2

Ethernet version 2 was last updated in November 1982. Since that time, all of Ethernet related efforts have been focused through the IEEE 802.3 subcommittee. In reality (actual application), the only differences are semantic in nature. Ethernet version 2 details are provided for historical perspective and reference only.

### 3.3.1 Collision Presence Signal and Collision Presence Test

A signal called the Collision Presence Signal (CPS) was introduced with Ethernet version 1 and carried into Ethernet version 2. This signal is generated by the transceiver to indicate the presence of multiple transmission attempts.

After every frame is sent, the Collision Presence Test (CPT) is transmitted by the transceiver on the collision signal wires of the AUI cable (the AUI is detailed in Chapter 5.) The transmission of this signal tests the collision detection circuitry. This signal became known as the heartbeat signal.

### 3.3.2 Ethernet Version 2 Frame Format

The Ethernet version 2 frame consists of five fields. These fields are, in order: the destination address, source address, type, data, and frame check sequence. The structure of the frame is depicted in Fig. 3.1. The minimum valid frame size is 64 bytes (512 bits) and the maximum valid frame size is 1518 bytes (12144 bits). Before each frame is sent, an 8-byte preamble signal is transmitted.

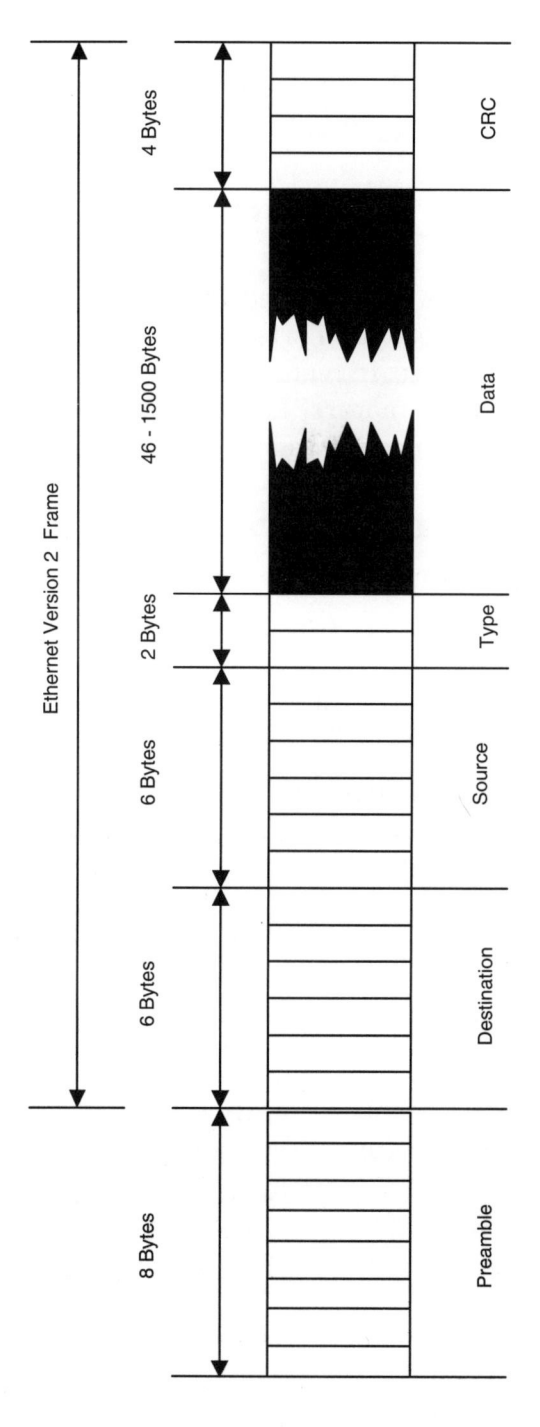

**Figure 3.1:** Ethernet version 2 frame

### 3.3 Ethernet Version 2

## 3.3.3 Preamble

When the data link layer presents a frame for transmission, the physical layer transmits a preamble signal. The preamble signal is a 64-bit pattern that is alternating 1s and 0s until the last two bits, which are both 1s. The generation of this signal provides the channel circuitry with the ability to be prepared for the frame that will follow. The preamble pattern is

```
10101010 10101010 10101010 10101010 10101010 10101010 10101010 10101011
```

The physical channel monitors the line looking for the double-one sequence at the end of the preamble. When the channel sees the double-one pattern, it then begins passing all subsequent bits to the data link layer.

## 3.3.4 Destination Address

The destination address contains the 6-byte (48-bit) Ethernet address of the intended destination(s). It may be a *physical* or *multicast* address.

The physical address is a unique address that corresponds to a specific station on the Ethernet.

A multicast address is an address that corresponds with one or more specific stations on the Ethernet. There are two types of multicast addresses defined in the Ethernet version 2 specification: the *multicast group address* and the *broadcast address*.

A multicast group address is an address that corresponds to a group of logically related stations that is defined by some higher level convention.

A broadcast address is a predefined multicast address that corresponds to all of the stations on the Ethernet.

### 3.3.5 Source Address

The source address contains a 6-byte (48-bit) Ethernet address of the transmitting source.

### 3.3.6 Type Field

The type field contains a 2-byte (16-bit) value. This value is not used at the Data Link layer; it is used at higher levels to identify the *Client Layer protocol* associated with the frame.

The Client Layer protocol refers to the collection of the higher network architecture that will use the Data Link layer (IP and IPX for example).

### 3.3.7 Data Field

The data field contains the data being sent with a minimum of 46 bytes (368 bits) and a maximum of 1500 bytes (12,000 bits). This field might contain data from a file that is being sent from one system to another. If the file being transmitted is larger than 1500 bytes, then multiple frames will be sent. The data in this field are totally transparent to the Data Link layer.

### 3.3.8 Frame Check Sequence (FCS)

The Frame Check Sequence (FCS) is a 4-byte (32-bit) field containing a mathematically produced figure, which represents the checksum value of the frame and is used to detect transmission errors. The value is computed as a function of the contents of all of the fields contained in the frame except the frame check sequence field. The frame check sequence is also known as the Cyclic Redundancy Check (CRC).

# 3.4 IEEE 802.3 Standard

It should be noted that the IEEE 802.3 standard is now synonymous with Ethernet. It is a networking standard developed by the IEEE, based on the CSMA/CD aspects of the Ethernet version 2 standard. As stated earlier, the only real differences are semantic.

## 3.4.1 Signal Quality Error (SQE)

As the IEEE adopted the Ethernet version 2 standards into their 802.3 standard, the Collision Presence Signal and the Collision Presence Test were renamed as the Signal Quality Error (SQE) and the test signals.

## 3.4.2 IEEE 802.3 Standard Frame Format

The IEEE 802.3 standard frame consists of seven fields. These fields are, in order: the preamble, start frame delimiter, destination address, source address, length, data, and frame check sequence. The structure of the frame is depicted in Fig. 3.2. It should be noted that the preamble field and the Start Frame Delimiter (SFD) field, when combined, are exactly the same as the Ethernet version 2 preamble.

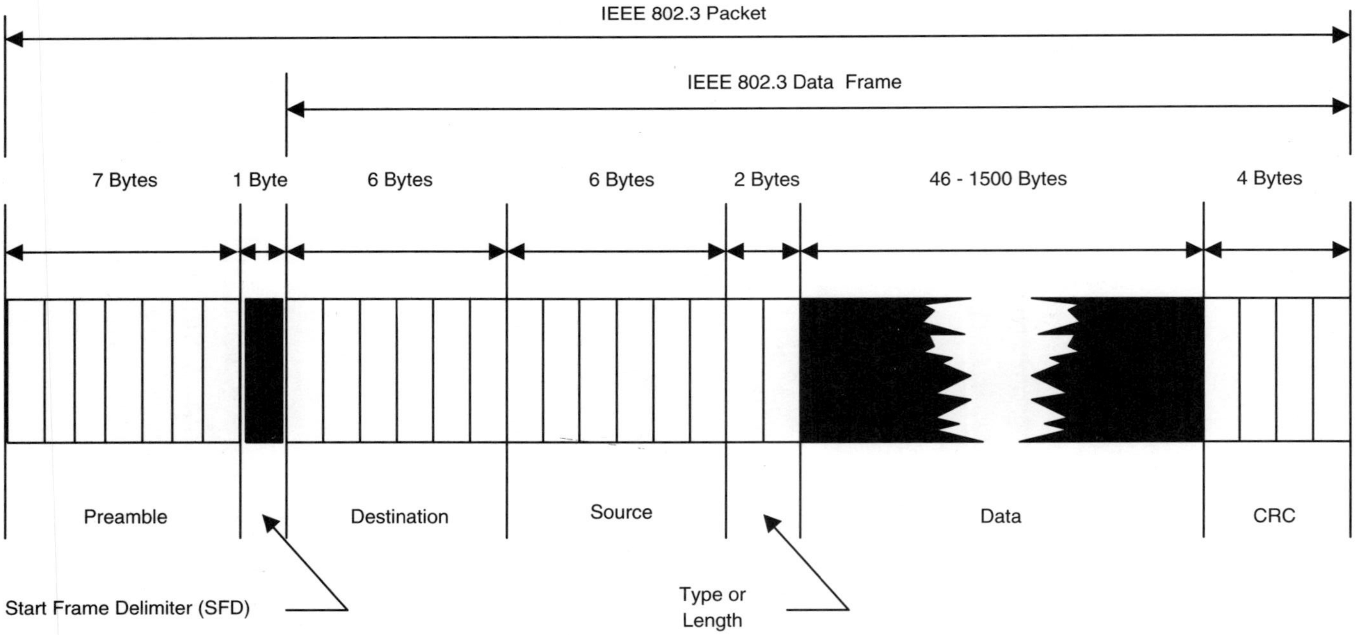

**Figure 3.2:** IEEE 802.3 packet

### 3.4.3 Preamble

The IEEE 802.3 standard envelopes the 7-byte (56-bit) preamble that is part of the normal transmission process of the Ethernet version 2 frame into its frame. Note that the preamble sent as part of a normal Ethernet version 2 transmission is not part of its defined frame structure and that it is eight bytes (64 bits). The first seven of these 7-bytes match up with the 7-bytes that make up the defined preamble field of the IEEE 802.3 standard.

### 3.4.4 Start Frame Delimiter (SFD)

The eighth byte of the Ethernet version 2 preamble is matched by the start frame delimiter field. This field is always the same 8-bit pattern, 10101011, and it indicates the beginning of the frame.

### 3.4.5 Destination Address

The destination address contains the 6-byte (48-bit) Ethernet address of the intended destination(s). It may be either a physical or multicast address, as described earlier.

### 3.4.6 Source Address

The source address contains the 6-byte (48-bit) Ethernet address of the station sending the frame.

### 3.4.7 Length Field / Type Field

This field can be either a type field of the same characteristics of the Ethernet version 2 type field or a length field (this is part of the 1997 802.3x supplement to the IEEE 802.3 standard).

The length field is a 2-byte (16-bit) field that indicates the number of Logical Link Control (LLC) bytes in the data field of the frame. The LLC bytes will be explained in Chapter 5.

### 3.4.8 Data Field

The data field contains the data being sent with a minimum of 46 bytes (368 bits) and a maximum of 1500 bytes (12,000 bits). This field might contain data from a file being transferred from one system to another. If the file being transmitted is larger than 1500 bytes, then multiple frames will be sent. The data in this field are totally transparent to the Data Link layer.

### 3.4.9 Frame Check Sequence

The frame check sequence is a 4-byte (32-bit) field containing a mathematically produced figure that represents the checksum value of the frame and is used to detect transmission errors. The value is computed as a function of the contents of all of the fields contained in the frame except the frame check sequence field. This field is also known as the CRC.

## 3.5 Chapter Summary

In this chapter three Ethernet specifications—Ethernet version 1, Ethernet version 2, and the IEEE 802.3—have been discussed.

## 3.6 Major Concepts

Ethernet version 1 is an obsolete standard and was never implemented by any major manufacturer.

The differences between Ethernet version 2 and the IEEE 802.3 specification are semantic.

The first difference is that the Ethernet version 2 specification preamble is an 8-byte signal, whereas the IEEE 802.3 wraps this signal into two field specifications—the preamble field, 7-bytes, and the start frame delimiter field, 1-byte. The bit stream, function, and purpose are exactly the same in both specifications.

Another difference is that the third field of the Ethernet version 2 frame and the fifth field in the IEEE 802.3 specification frame (which would be corresponding fields) can be used differently. In the Ethernet version 2 specification, the 2-byte field is used to provide information about the associated protocol to the client layer. In the IEEE 802.3 specification it can be used for the same purpose or to indicate how many LLC bytes are in the data field of the frame.

Lastly, a third significant difference is that in the Ethernet version 2 specification, the only defined transmission speed was 10Mbps. With the IEEE 802.3 specification, both 10Mbps and 100Mbps are currently specified, and there is activity to add a 1Gbps addendum. However, this is due to the fact that work on the Ethernet version 2 specification stopped in 1982 and all subsequent efforts were given to the IEEE 802.3 specifications.

CHAPTER 3                                                      *Ethernet Versions*

## 3.7 Vocabulary

### Broadcast Address

A predefined multicast address that corresponds to all of the stations on the network.

### Destination Address

The 6-byte (48-bit) Ethernet address of the intended destination(s). It may be a *physical* or *multicast* address.

### Multicast Address or Multicast Group Address

An address that corresponds with one or more specific stations on the Ethernet. There are two types of multicast addresses defined in the Ethernet version 2 specification: the *multicast group address* and the *broadcast address*.

### Physical Address

A unique address that corresponds to a specific station on the Ethernet.

# 3.8 Chapter 3 Review Questions

1. What information is contained in the basic Ethernet version 2 frame?

2. What is the difference between the Ethernet version 2 frame and the IEEE 802.3 frame?

3. Define the source address field.

4. Define the destination address field.

5. What is a multicast address?

# Chapter 4

# 10Mbps Ethernet

## 4.1 Introduction

Ethernet versions 1 and 2 and the IEEE 802.3 standard were all introduced in Chapter 3. Since 1985 the IEEE 802.3 standard has been the default choice, as it is the standard to which manufacturers have produced their equipment. The IEEE 802.3 standard has become synonymous with Ethernet. After this point, whenever the word Ethernet is used, it will be assumed that the IEEE 802.3 standard is being discussed (unless otherwise noted).

There are four media types defined for use with 10Mbps Ethernet:

- Thick coax (10BASE5)
- Thin coax (10BASE2)
- Twisted pair (10BASE-T)
- Fiber optic (10BASE-F)

All of these implementations use the same CSMA/CD medium access control protocol discussed in Chapter 2.

The IEEE identifiers for each of the media types can be read as follows: The first part of the identifier, "10," stands for 10Mbps, the transmission speed. The second part, "BASE," indicates baseband, meaning that only one signal can be broadcast on the medium at a time without interference. Finally, the third part indicates the type of medium. The "5" stands for 500 meters, the maximum length for thick coax, the "2" stands for thin coax (200 meters), the "T" stands for twisted pair, and the "F" stands for fiber optic. These different types of media will be discussed in greater detail in Chapter 6.

## 4.2 Data Link Layer

The data link layer is divided into two functional control sublayers: the Logical Layer Control (LLC), and the Media Access Control (MAC).

The IEEE has a separate sublayer called the IEEE 802.2 Logical Link Control—the MAC sublayer is defined in the IEEE 802.3 specification.

### 4.2.1 Logical Link Control (LLC)

There are two implementations of the LLC: LLC-1, and LLC-2. LLC-1 is used with Appletalk, and LLC-2 is used by IBM (NetBios). If the LLC is used, it indicates that the third field in the data frame is being

## 4.2 Data Link Layer

used as a type field. If it is not used, it indicates that this field is being used as a type field. Other than Appletalk and IBM (NetBios), LLC is rarely, if ever, used.

The LLC sublayer connects the client layer to the MAC sublayer and is responsible for the generation and interpretation of the commands that control data flow and, in the LLC-2 implementation, performs recovery procedures in the event of errors.

The LLC sublayer appends one byte of information about the destination client layer process, called the Destination Service Access Point (DSAP), and one byte about the source client layer process, called the Source Service Access Point (SSAP), to the data provided by the client layer for transmission on the LAN. This combined information is termed a Protocol Data Unit (PDU) and a control field.

The most important fact about the LLC is that it is rarely used with Ethernet. It is much more prevalent with Token Ring.

### 4.2.2 Media Access Control (MAC)

As defined in Chapter 2, the MAC is a set of rules that control access to the LAN for the transmission of data. The concept of Carrier Sense Multiple Access with Collision Detection (CSMA/CD), described in Chapter 2, is one major function of the MAC sublayer.

The MAC sublayer is also responsible for moving data on and off the LAN. Movement of data on and off the LAN entails two major areas: addressing and frame handling.

## Addressing

Each node connecting to the LAN is assigned its own unique physical address. This address is called the MAC address. The MAC address is determined by a chip on the network interface electronics. Ethernet uses a 6-byte (48-bit) MAC address. The address representation can take several forms. The four most common are shown below:

```
0800091b0054    0800.091b.0054    08:00:09:1b:00:54    Ä08-00-09-1b-00-54
```

\* Note that each digit in the address is hexadecimal.

‡ This is the standard representation.

The first bit is reserved for use in the destination address field to indicate if the destination address is an individual or a group address. If this bit is set to 0, then the intended receiver is an individual address. If the bit is 1, then the destination is a group of addresses (multicast or broadcast). Address definitions were provided in Chapter 3.

The second bit is reserved to distinguish between globally or locally administered addresses. If this bit is set to 0, then it is for a globally administered address. When this bit is set to 1, it indicates a locally administered address, unless it is a broadcast (note all 48 bits must be 1 for a broadcast).

The first three bytes of the address are reserved for an organization code. For example, Hewlett-Packard has a unique organization code of 08:00:09, as well as many others.

The remaining 3 bytes are used to identify the unique address of that network interface by the manufacturer.

## *Frame Handling*

When a node transmits data, the MAC accepts that data from the client layers and builds a frame by attaching the preamble, start frame delimiter, destination address, source address, and length or type field to the beginning of the data. In addition, the MAC calculates the final frame size. If it is less than 64 bytes, it also appends PAD characters to the end of the data. With the frame constructed, the MAC then performs the CSMA/CD functions described in Chapter 2. As the frame is transmitted, the CRC is calculated and appended as the FCS field to the end of the frame.

When receiving frames, the MAC is responsible for not accepting frames that are not addressed to the receiving node and moving frames that are addressed to the receiving node into a buffer. With the frame captive, the MAC calculates the CRC and verifies that the frame is valid. It then strips the preamble, start frame delimiter, destination and source addresses, length fields, and any PAD characters from the frame and passes the data to the LLC sublayer.

## 4.2.3 Physical Layer

At the physical layer of the 10Mbps specifications there are two major compatibility interfaces defined. These are the Medium Dependent Interface (MDI) and the Attachment Unit Interface (AUI). These two interfaces are also two of the components of the five Ethernet physical layer building blocks.

## 4.2.4 Ethernet Physical Layer Building Blocks

Working from the physical medium to the network node, there are five specific building blocks used to construct the Ethernet connection. They are the physical medium, the Medium Dependent Interface (MDI), the Medium Attachment Unit (MAU), the Attachment Unit Interface (AUI), and the Data Terminal Equipment (DTE).

## 4.2.5 Physical Medium

The physical medium is the cable that actually carries the Ethernet signal. In the Ethernet specification, this cable can be thick coax, thin coax, twisted pair, or optical fiber. Currently, the most common medium is twisted pair. Each type of cable has its own package of benefits and liabilities. All of these cables are discussed in detail in Chapter 6.

## 4.2.6 Medium Dependent Interface (MDI)

Connecting the physical medium to a network device requires connectors appropriate to make the physical and electrical connection. This connection is accomplished through hardware with specific characteristics for the medium and electrical connection. This hardware is called the Medium Dependent Interface (MDI) because, depending on the medium, the electrical connection and supporting hardware will change. The MDI for 10BASE-T is an RJ45, while the MDI for 10BASE2 is a BNC connector.

In the 10BASE5 specification, where the thick coax is used, a special clamp type connector called a vampire tap is common. This connector clamps onto the thick coaxial cable and then utilizes an invasive tap to bore through the outer sheath and braid the inner insulator to make a connection to the center conductor of the coax. This vampire tap arrangement would obviously not work for twisted pair or fiber optic cables and was not employed for use with the thin coax cable. Therefore, it was "dependent" on the thick coax.

## 4.2.7 Medium Attachment Unit (MAU)

The Medium Attachment Unit (MAU) utilizes the MDI to connect to the physical medium and transmits and receives signals to and from the physical medium. The MAU is often referred to as a transceiver.

The MAU can be either an external or internal device. The typical external device is a self-contained unit with an Attachment Unit Interface (AUI) connection and an appropriate MDI. The MAU can also be integrated into the controller circuitry so that there is no visible external connection other than the MDI.

## 4.2.8 Attachment Unit Interface (AUI)

The next piece in the connection is the Attachment Unit Interface (AUI). The AUI carries the signals from the MAU to the Data Terminal Equipment (DTE). The most common implementation is a cable. However, the cable can be eliminated if the MAU will connect directly to the back of the network node. The AUI cable is commonly referred to as a transceiver cable.

## 4.2.9 Data Terminal Equipment (DTE)

The network node is called the Data Terminal Equipment (DTE). This is another term that finds its roots in the history of computer science. The DTE contains the required hardware and software to perform the

CHAPTER 4                                                      *10Mbps Ethernet*

Media Access Control (MAC) functions necessary to send and receive Ethernet frames in what is called the Ethernet interface.

## 4.2.10 Building Blocks Summary

The typical connection would then be represented by the block diagram in Fig. 4.1. The Ethernet frames are carried on the physical medium as electrical signals. The physical medium is then connected to the appropriate MDI, which in turn is connected to the MAU, which is connected to the AUI, whether internal or external to the network node, and finally the connection is made to the DTE.

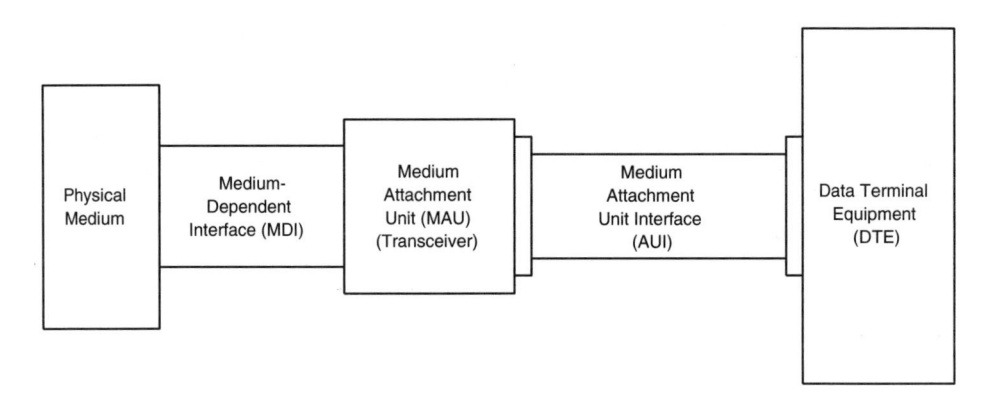

**Figure 4.1:** 10Mbps Ethernet building blocks

## 4.3 Chapter Summary

This chapter has discussed 10Mpbs Ethernet in terms of the data link layer and the physical layer.

### 4.3.1 Major Concepts

The data link layer is split into two parts: the Logical Link Control (LLC) and the Media Access Control (MAC) sublayers.

If present, the LLC receives the data to be sent to the remote network node from the client layer. The LLC attaches the appropriate 1-byte code for the destination client layer process (Destination Service Access Point or DSAP), the appropriate 1-byte code for the originating client layer process (Source Service Access Point or SSAP), and the one or two bytes of control information. The final unit of combined information produced by the LLC sublayer—the DSAP, SSAP, control, and data from the client layer—is called the LLC Protocol Data Unit (PDU). The LLC is rarely implemented in Ethernet.

The MAC receives the LLC PDU, or the data from the client layer, and attaches the 7-byte preamble—1-byte start frame delimiter, the 6-byte destination and source MAC addresses, and the length field to the beginning. If there are less than 46 bytes in the data field, a PAD of characters is provided to insure that the final frame meets the minimal valid frame size of 64 bytes. The CSMA/CD media contention methodology is applied and the frame is sent to the remote station. The CRC calculation is performed as the frame is transmitted and the results are appended in the 4-byte FCS field after the transmission of the final bit of the data field. The result is the final Ethernet frame.

In reverse, the MAC sublayer receives the intended frame by moving it into the buffer. The MAC sublayer then strips off the preamble, start frame delimiter, length and frame check sequence fields and passes the remaining data to the LLC sublayer, or client layer.

The physical layer is constructed from five building blocks: the physical medium, Medium Dependent Interface (MDI), the Medium Attachment Unit Interface (MAU), Attachment Unit Interface (AUI), and Data Terminal Equipment (DTE).

## 4.4 Vocabulary

### LLC

Logical Link Control sublayer. Moves data from the client layer to the MAC layer after appending DSAP, SSAP, and any required pad characters. Rarely implemented in Ethernet.

### DSAP

Destination Service Access Point. The 1-byte code that identifies the destination client layer process.

*4.4 Vocabulary*

## SSAP

Source Service Access Point. The 1-byte code that identifies the source client layer process.

## MAC

Media Access Control sublayer. A set of rules that control access to the LAN for the transmission of data.

## MDI

Medium Dependent Interface. The interface hardware that is specific to, or dependent upon, a specific medium.

## MAU

Medium Attachment Unit. Transmits and receives signals to and from the transmission medium. Often called a transceiver.

## AUI

Attachment Unit Interface. The connection between the MAU and the Data Terminal Equipment (DTE).

## DTE

Data Terminal Equipment. The required hardware and software to perform MAC functions for the transmission and reception of data.

## 4.5 Chapter 4 Review Questions

1. Name the five Ethernet building blocks.

2. What are the physical media for Ethernet?

3. What is the MDI?

4. What is the MAU?

5. What is the AUI?

6. What is the DTE?

7. What is another term for transceiver?

# Chapter 5

# Fast Ethernet

## 5.1 Introduction

The IEEE has continued to make improvements to its standard, while the Ethernet version 2 standard was completed and published in November of 1982. There have been significant changes in the IEEE 802.3 standard over the years. One of the most significant changes came with the addition of Section 14 (Twisted-Pair MAU and Baseband Medium Type 10BASE-T), which was published in 1990.

The continuation of improvement of the IEEE 802.3 standard and its dominance in the market has resulted in a blur of terminology. When the term Fast Ethernet is used, it refers to improvements in the IEEE 802.3 standards that allow the transmission speed to increase from 10Mbps to 100Mbps.

The 100BASE-T standard consists of five separate specifications: Media Access Control (MAC), Medium Independent Interface (MII), and four physical layers (100BASE-TX, 100BASE-T4, 100BASE-T2, and 100BASE-FX.)

## 5.2 Modifications to the 802.3 Standard

Fast Ethernet is a supplement to the 802.3 standard as it already exists. The 10Mbps 802.3 specifications are contained in the IEEE Standard 802.3a through 802.3t, clauses 1 through 20. Fast Ethernet is simply the 100Mpbs 802.3 standard found in the IEEE standard 802.3u, clauses 21 through 30.

The authors of Fast Ethernet were very interested in guaranteeing the backwards compatibility between both the old, 802.3a-t, and the new 802.3u standards. The best example of the effort to provide guaranteed interoperability is clause 28 (Auto-Negotiation). This clause, discussed in greater detail later in this chapter, allows 10BASE-T and Fast Ethernet devices to recognize one another and automatically negotiate an acceptable operating speed.

To better understand the new specifications, a brief overview of each clause will be presented. The details of 100BASe-T4, 100BASE-TX, and 100BASE-FX will be covered in Chapters 6 and 7.

## 5.3 Clause 21—100BASE-T Introduction

The 100BASE-T introduction is formally known as clause 21. The two functions of the 100BASE-T introduction are to first place the 100BASE-T clauses in reference to the OSI model, which was discussed in Chapter 1, and, second, provide common information to all of the 100BASE-T clauses.

### 5.3.1 100BASE-T Clauses in Relation to the OSI Model

Clauses 21 and 29 are related to the OSI model Layer 2, the data link layer. Clauses 22 through 28 are related to the physical layer of the OSI model, Layer 1. Section 30 is not related to the OSI model.

### 5.3.2 Common Information

The abbreviations and terms used in the Protocol Implementation Conformance Statements (PICS) are a major part of clause 21. Also included in this clause are state diagrams and explanations of how to interpret them.

## 5.4 Clause 22—Media Independent Interface (MII)

While the 10Mbps AUI standard is the standard for 10Mbps, it is replaced in the 100Mpbs specification by two parts—the Medium Independent Interface (MII) and the reconciliation sublayer of clause 22.

### 5.4.1 Medium Independent Interface (MII)

The function of the MII is to provide the specifications for the signal, connectors, and cable lengths that interconnect the MAC and the Physical Layer Entity (PHY). The PHY is the new term for transceiver and replaces MAU. The MII utilizes a 40-pin connector to provide signal connectivity.

Another additional feature of the MII is the new two-wire serial bus called the management interface. The purpose of this simple interface is to provide a mechanism for the adapter card to gather information from the transceiver.

### 5.4.2 Reconciliation Sublayer

The reconciliation sublayer is a translation layer that provides the interface from the MAC to the MII. Signals are passed between the MII and the MAC and vice versa through this layer. This sublayer is not configurable and has no other user definable options.

It is notable that this layer is an architectural abstraction that does not have a physical implementation (see Fig. 5.1).

## 5.4 Clause 22—Media Independent Interface (MII)

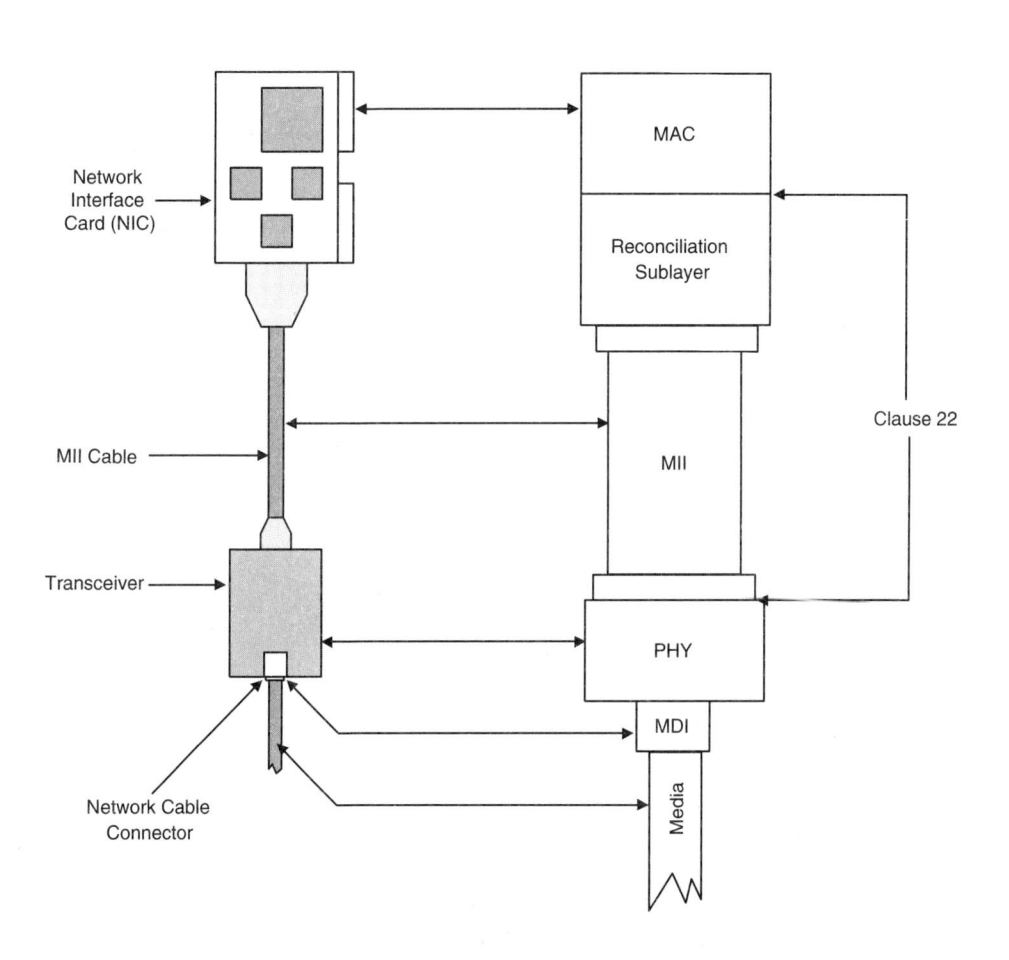

**Figure 5.1:** Clause 22 terms in relation to physical hardware

CHAPTER 5                                           *Fast Ethernet*

## 5.5 Clause 23—100BASE-T4 Transceiver

This clause consists of two functional areas: the Physical Coding Sublayer (PCS) and the Physical Medium Attachment (PMA).

The PCS handles data coding, error checking, and collision detection. When data is to be transmitted, 100BASE-T4 codes the data with a method called 8B6T coding. This is done to make it less expensive to produce a product that meets the radio-frequency emissions tests which are required internationally. Simply put, the 8B6T coding spreads the data transmitted onto three pairs which reduces the effective transmission rate of each pair to 33.33 Mb/s for the total effective transmission rate of 100 MB/s.

The PMA provides link integrity carrier detection and error detection. The link integrity function in the PMA provides the ability to detect a failure of the wiring. Upon detection of a wiring failure the link integrity function disables the transceiver.

### 5.5.1 Physical Details

100BASE-T4 can use category 3, 4, or 5 Unshielded Twisted Pair (UTP) cabling.

The T4 transceiver performs its functions in a very different manner than the other IEEE 802.3 twisted pair schemes. In the T4 methodology, there are four pairs of wires. One pair is dedicated to transmit, one pair is dedicated to receive, and two are bidirectional. The transmitted data is then spread across three pairs of the cable, reducing the bandwidth requirement for each pair.

*5.5 Clause 23—100BASE-T4 Transceiver*

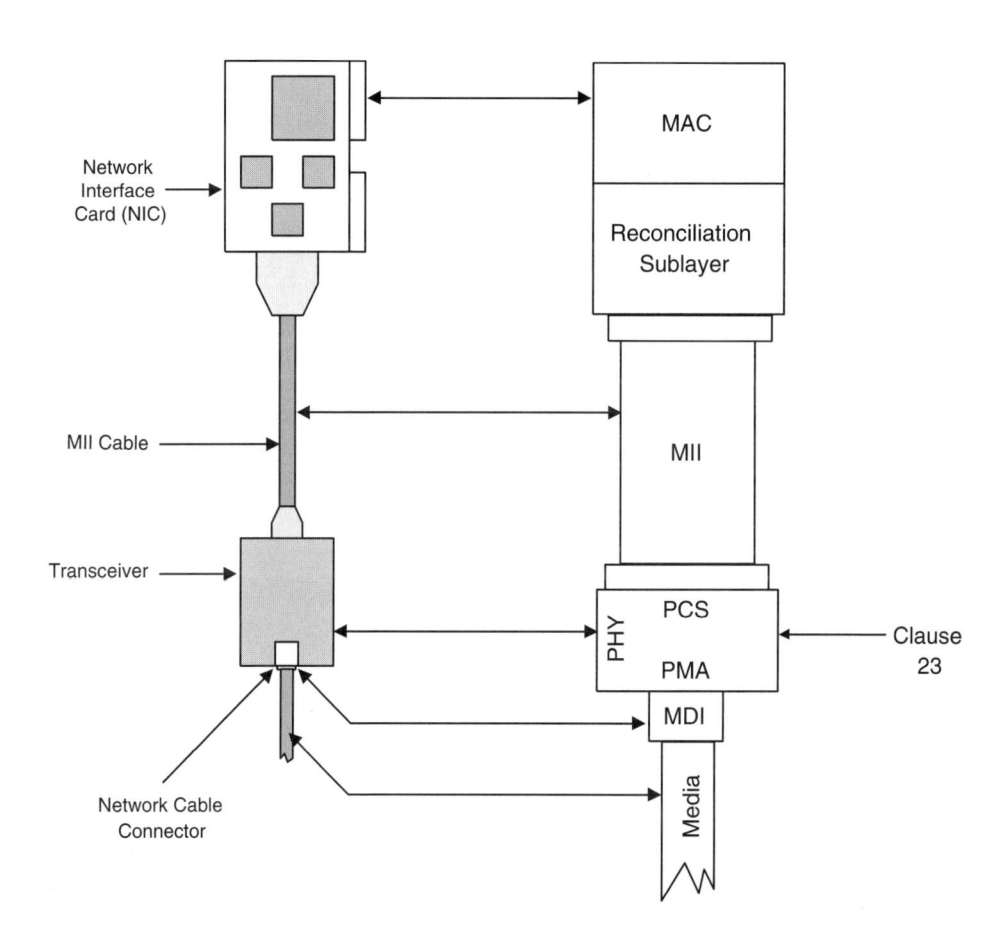

**Figure 5.2:** Clause 23 terms in relation to physical hardware

### 5.5.2 Physical Coding Sublayer (PCS)

The PCS for 100BASE-T4 uses a data coding scheme called 8B6T. In this coding scheme, data is received in nibbles (4 bits) from the MII. These nibbles are paired into octets (8 bits). The octets are in turn transmitted onto each of the three pairs in a round-robin method.

This style of coding uses ternary signals in place of binary. The signals are transmitted ternary, meaning that they have three states. This type of signal can provide more information per clock cycle than a binary signal can with its two states. Couple this ternary signaling with the effective data rate for each pair being 33.33MHz (one-third of 100MHz) and the fact that the ternary signaling rate is three-quarters of the 33.33MHz, which happens to be 25MHz. This is a significant frequency because it is the clock frequency of the MII, which means that there is no additional transmit clock circuitry required.

## 5.6 Clause 24— 100BASE-X Transceiver

Clause 24, or the 100BASE-X transceiver, is the base for the TX and FX transceivers. This clause defines much of the same functionality as clause 23 in that it is also defined by a PCS and PMA sublayer. The major difference between clauses 23 and 24 is that clause 23 stands on its own as a functional transceiver, while clause 24 requires the addition of the Physical Media Dependent (PMD) sublayer of either

*5.8 Clause 26—FX PMD*

clause 25, for a functional 100BASE-TX transceiver, or the PMD of clause 26, for a functional 100BASE-FX transceiver.

In both the TX and FX transceivers, the analog functions are provided by the Physical Media Dependent (PMD) sublayer of the corresponding clause.

## 5.7 Clause 25—TX PMD

The specifics of the connectors, wiring, and signal levels contained in the PMD sublayer for the twisted pair (TX) component of the 100BASE-TX transceiver are defined in clause 25. This specification of low-level analog functionality combined with the functionality described in clause 24 make up the fully functional specifications for the 100BASE-TX transceiver.

## 5.8 Clause 26—FX PMD

Clause 26 specifies connectors, wiring, and signal levels contained in the PMD sublayer for the fiber-optic (FX) component of the 100BASE-FX transceiver. This specification of low-level analog functionality, along with the functionality described in clause 24, make up the fully functional specifications for the 100BASE-FX transceiver (see Fig. 5.3).

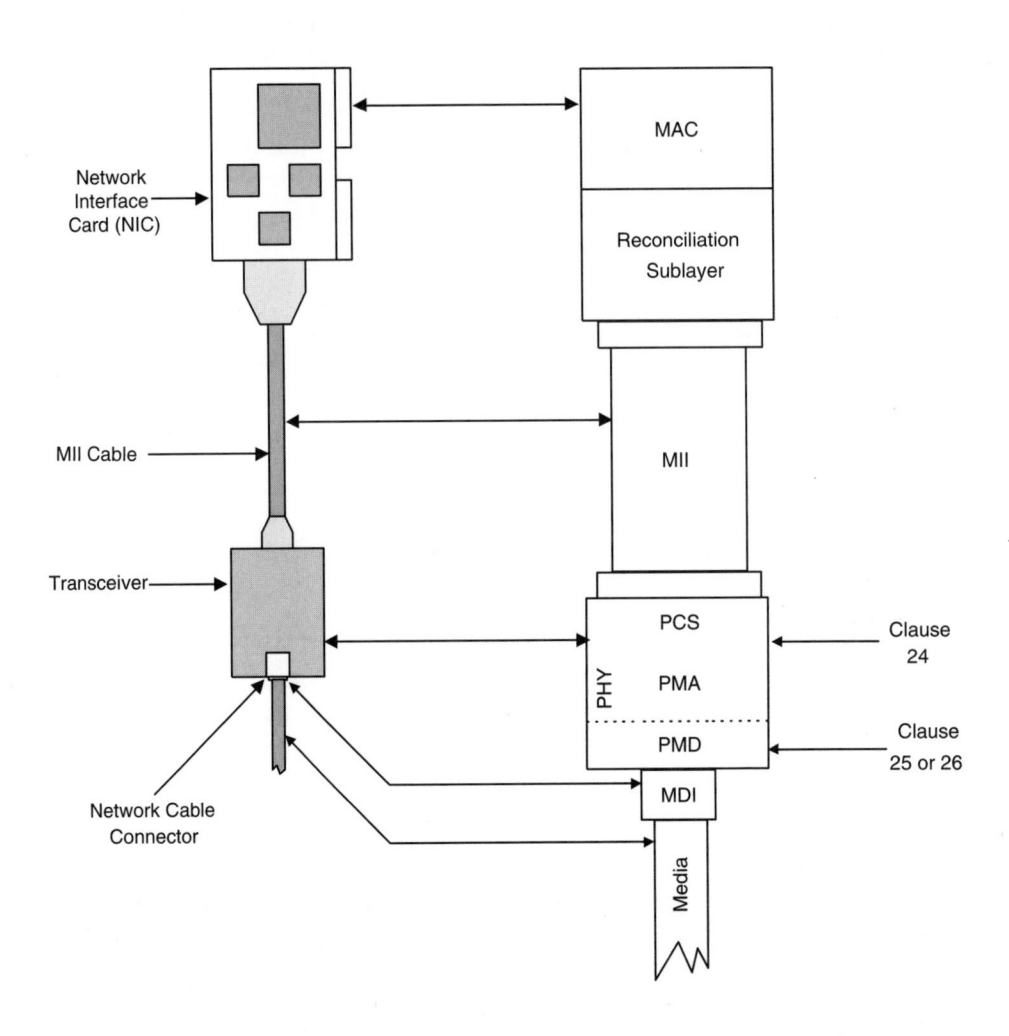

**Figure 5.3:** Clauses 24, 25 and 26 in relation to physical hardware

## 5.9 Clause 27—Repeaters

This clause defines repeater types and functionality for Fast Ethernet. Detailed information regarding hardware is provided in Chapter 6.

## 5.10 Clause 28—Auto-Negotiation

Auto-negotiation provides a method for a Network Interface Card (NIC) or hub that is configured with both 10Mpbs and 100Mbps interfaces, which automatically sense the speed of the network and adapt to it, as long as the network is 802.3 compliant. This provides a significant benefit to the company that installs dual speed cards on a 10BASE-T network and then decides to upgrade a piece at a time to 100BASE-T.

## 5.11 Clause 29—Topology

This clause defines rules in regard to the concept known as the collision domain. A collision domain is simply a network in which there will be a collision if two or more nodes transmit at the same time. Chapter 6 will show that bridges, switches, and routers work to partition networks into multiple subnetworks, each becoming their own collision domain.

## 5.12 Clause 30—Management

The field of network management is no longer new. It is a very extensive field. The management clause of Fast Ethernet deals with a very small portion of network management called Management Information dataBase or MIB. The MIB is simply a specification for the management agent to use to handle commands, report status, count events, and generate alarms.

The original MIB specifications for 10Mbps Ethernet were found in clauses 5, 19, and 20 of the 802.3 standard. All of these have now been subsumed into and superseded by clause 30.

There are MIBs for many network products on the market today. However, there are no manufacturers that adhere to the IEEE standards with regards to management of network resources. The IETF/SNMP standards are considered more important in this regard and are the blueprint for most management products.

## 5.13 Summary

In this chapter, it has been clearly identified that the Fast Ethernet specifications, as provided by the IEEE, are located in the 802.3u supplement in clauses 21 through 30. Each of these clauses handles a specific portion of the functional specification.

*5.13 Summary*

## 5.13.1 Major Concepts

The major component of Ethernet, which is the MAC concept of CSMA/CD, has not changed in this specification. The definition of the frame has also remained the same. This provides a level of compatibility across the 10 and 100Mbps specifications.

There was great interest in guaranteeing the interoperability between both the old supplements, 802.3a-t, and the new supplement, 802.3u, standards. The best example of the effort to provide guaranteed interoperability is clause 28 (auto-negotiation). This clause permits 10BASE-T and Fast Ethernet devices to recognize one another and automatically negotiate an acceptable operating speed.

The 10Mbps AUI standard is replaced by two parts—the Medium Independent Interface (MII) and the reconciliation sublayer of clause 22.

The specification for the 100BASE-T4 transceiver is notably different from the 100BASE-TX transceiver in three major ways.

- The 100BASE-T4 clause (clause 23) defines a functional transceiver, while the 100BASE-TX transceiver requires the combination of both clauses 24 and 25.
- The signaling methodology is different. The 100BASE-T4 specification calls for one pair to be dedicated for transmit, one pair to be dedicated for receive, and two pairs to be bidirectional. The transmitted data is then spread across three pairs of the cable, reducing the bandwidth requirement and load for each pair. This bandwidth reduction results in the ability to recover from errors more easily, which in turn results in a more robust network.

- The 100BASE-T4 PHY is divided into two sublayers: the PCS and the PMA. The 100BASE-TX PHY includes the addition of a third sublayer, the PMD.

There is a major difference in the PMA sublayer of the T4 and TX transceivers and all of the other IEEE 802.3 standard transceivers. The major difference is that the T4 and TX transceivers do not use the SQE test or jabber signal. The T4 and TX transceivers do not require the SQE test because it uses the link integrity function to make sure that it can receive signals from the far end and because the MII performs a special test to verify functionality of the collision-detect wire.

## 5.14 Vocabulary

### MII

Medium Independent Interface. The specifications for the signal, connectors, and cable lengths that interconnect the MAC and PHY.

### PCS

Physical Coding Sublayer.

### PHY

Physical Layer Entity. It replaced the 10Mbps MAU.

## PMA

Physical Media Attachment sublayer.

## PMD

Physical Media Dependent sublayer. The specifics of the connectors, wiring, and signal levels for a medium.

## Reconciliation Sublayer

A translation layer that provides the interface from the MAC to the MII. Signals are passed between the MII and the MAC and vice versa through this layer. This sublayer is not configurable and has no other user definable options.

# 5.15 Chapter 5 Review Questions

1. What is a significant difference between clause 23 and clause 24?

2. What are two unique things found in the 100BASE-T4 specification?

3. What physical hardware does the MAC correspond to?

4. What is the MII?

5. What physical hardware does the PHY correspond to?

6. What is the MDI?

7. What physical hardware does the MDI correspond to?

# Chapter 6

# 100BASE-T2, T4, and TX

## 6.1 Introduction

The most popular Fast Ethernet technologies are the 100BASE-T series. As stated earlier in Chapter 5, the introduction to 100BASE-T is contained in clause 21, with following clauses defining the interfaces, transceivers, and other information. In this chapter, we will go into deeper detail regarding the configuration of the 100BASE-T technologies.

## 6.2 100BASE-T Media

100BASE-TX technology can use either shielded or unshielded twisted pair cabling. 100BASE-T2 and T4 specify unshielded twisted pair cable. Unshielded Twisted Pair (UTP) cabling is by far the most popular medium. The 100BASE-T2 and T4 technologies will permit the use of twisted pair cabling termed as a Category 3 level cable, while the 100BASE-TX technologies require twisted pair cable termed as a Category 5 (CAT5) cabling.

## 6.2.1 Twisted Pair

Twisted pair cables are cables that contain multiple pairs of wires, each of which are twisted. Each wire is insulated. The insulation is color coded to make identification of each wire and each wire pair easy.

The twisting of each pair is done to help reduce what is called cross talk, that is noise which is induced from one wire to other wires as data is transmitted. The twisting of each pair should continue as close as possible to the point where the cable is terminated with a connector. The maximum length of the untwisted pairs at the ends by the connectors is one-half inch.

## 6.2.2 Shielded and Unshielded Cables

There are two types of twisted pair cables that are acceptable for use—shielded and unshielded. The shielded cable has a braided shield, a foil shield, or both, which is just under the cable jacket, acting like a second cable jacket. The unshielded cable does not have the shield.

The most commonly used cable is unshielded twisted pair (UTP). UTP cable must have characteristic impedance of 100 ohms (W). While only 100BASE-TX requires cable rated as Category 5 cable and 100BASE-T2 and T4 can use Category 3 (CAT3) rated cable, it is best to install the Category 5 (CAT5) rated cable to all. Installing Category 5 cable will provide a higher quality twisted pair cabling infrastructure for a small increase in the cost of the cable.

Both the Category 3 and Category 5 cables are constructed from four pairs of unshielded, individually twisted 24 AWG (American Wire Gauge) wire.

The Shielded Twisted Pair (STP) cable allowed is 150W for 100BASE-TX.

### 6.2.3 Category 3 (CAT3) Cabling

The CAT3 cable is rated for transmission characteristics of 16Mhz. This simply means that it can handle up to 16 million bits of information on each pair of the cable. This is the minimum that is required for 100BASE-T2 and T4.

### 6.2.4 Category 5 (CAT5) Cabling

The CAT5 cable is rated at 100Mhz. This simply means that it can handle up to 1 million bits of information on each pair of the cable. This is required for 100BASE-TX and is highly recommended for 100BASE-T2 and T4 installations.

## 6.3 100BASE-T2

The 100BASE-T2 standards major components are the media and the Physical Layer (PHY), or transceiver, and repeaters.

### 6.3.1 100BASE-T2 Media

The 100BASE-T2 standards support the use of either Category 3 (CAT3) UTP or 120W STP cable. The recommendation is to use Cate-

| CHAPTER 6 | 100BASE-T2, T4, and TX |
|---|---|

gory 5 (CAT5) cable to provide a higher quality link, which will provide improvement in the reception of signals. In this section, all reference to cable will be CAT5. Four pairs are used: one pair for transmitting data (TX), one pair for receiving data (RX), and two pairs that are bidirectional (BI).

The maximum length of CAT5 cable is 100 meters. 100BASE-T2 is limited by round-trip timing specifications. This means that 100BASE-T2 has an absolute maximum of 100 meters. This length includes the cable used to connect the network device (computer for example) to the wall plate, the wall plate to the cross connect panel, and the cross connect panel to the repeater (see Fig. 6.1).

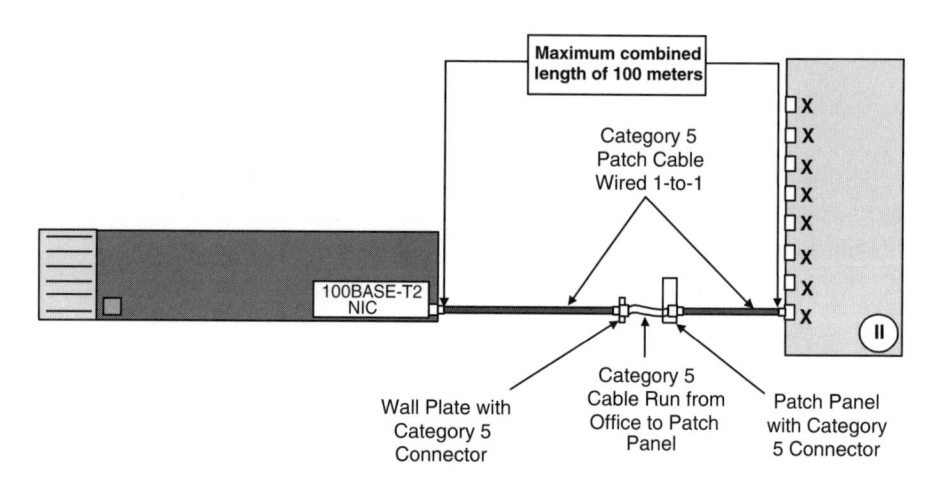

**Figure 6.1:** Simplified 100BASE-T2 connection to a repeater

To meet the CAT3 or CAT5 specifications requires more than just using CAT5 cabling. The connectors that terminate the cables and are

## 6.3 100BASE-T2

used in the wall plates and patch panels must all meet all CAT3 or CAT5 specifications to be effective.

The plug ends used to terminate the CAT3 or CAT5 cabling are 8-pin RJ-45 style connectors. The two pairs of wires required for 100BASE-T2 leave four of the eight pairs of the connector unused. However, all four of the pairs should be connected. Connecting all four pairs of the cable provides the ability to use a different technology later, like 100BASE-T4, without having to replace the cable ends. In the event that a crossover cable is required, it is recommended that the cable be wired as a 100BASE-T4 crossover. The two pairs required for 100BASE-T2 are wired exactly the same for 100BASE-T4 and 100BASE-TX. The only difference is the connection of the unused two pairs of wires are now configured properly for 100BASE-T4 (see Fig. 6.2).

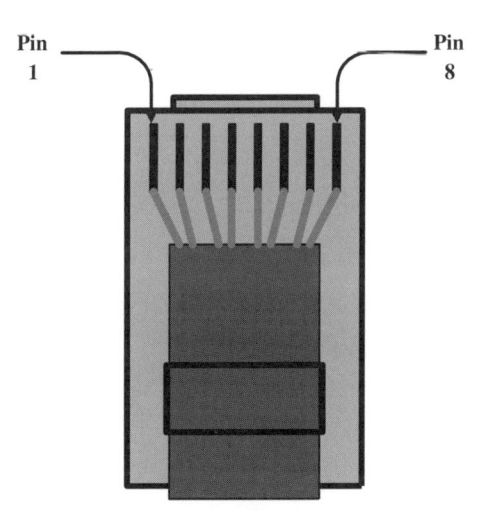

**Figure 6.2:** RJ-45 connector

The transmit and receive signals are now polarized by the positive signal carried on one of the wire pairs and the positive signal carried on the other.

## 6.4 100BASE-T2 Pin Assignments

1—TD+
2—TD-
3—RD+
4—Not Used
5—Not Used
6—RD-
7—Not Used
8—Not Used

## 6.5 100BASE-T2 Crossover

1—3
2—6
3—1
6—2

*6.5 100BASE-T2 Crossover*

The pin out for 10BASE-T is exactly the same. So if there are 10BASE-T line cords or patch cords available that meet the CAT3 or CAT5 specifications, they can be used.

## 6.5.1 100BASE-T2 Repeaters

There are two types of repeaters defined for use with 100BASE-T2: Class I and Class II. The repeaters must be labeled with either a I or II centered in a circle to indicate the class of the repeater.

### *Class I Repeater*

The Class I repeater translates the incoming signals to digital form and then retranslates them to line signals as they are sent back out. This permits the repeater to have 100BASE-TX, 100BASE-T2, 100BASE T4, and 100BASE-FX segments, which use different signaling techniques, connected. Only one Class I repeater should be used per collision domain.

### *Class II Repeater*

Class II repeaters are limited to repeating only like signals. This means that only 100BASE-TX and T2, or 100BASE-FX and 100BASE-T4, segments would appear on a single Class II router. This restriction results in smaller timing delays. The smaller timing delay means that a maximum of two Class II repeaters can be used in a given collision domain.

## 6.5.2 100BASE-T2 Link Integrity Check

The transceiver (PHY) circuitry monitors the receive data path for activity to determine if the link is operational. When there are no stations transmitting the 100BASE-T2, PHY transmits link pulses to assure link integrity. Called fast link pulses, these signals are used in conjunction with the auto-negotiation mechanism, allowing hubs that permit connection of both 10Mbps and 100Mbs to detect the speed of the link.

# 6.6 100BASE-T4

The 100BASE-T4 standards major components are the media and the Physical Layer (PHY), or transceiver, and repeaters.

## 6.6.1 100BASE-T4 Media

The 100BASE-T4 standards support the use of Category 3 (CAT3) UTP. The recommendation is to use Category 5 (CAT5) cable to provide a higher quality link, which will provide improvement in the reception of signals. In this section, all reference to cables will be CAT5. Four pairs are used: one pair for transmitting data (TX), one pair for receiving data (RX), and two pairs that are bidirectional (BI).

The maximum length of either CAT3 or CAT5 cable is 100 meters. 100BASE-T4 is limited by round-trip timing specifications. This means that 100BASE-T4 has an absolute maximum of 100 meters. This length includes the cable used to connect the network device (computer for

## 6.6 100BASE-T4

example) to the wall plate, the wall plate to the cross connect panel, and the cross connect panel to the repeater (see Fig. 6.3).

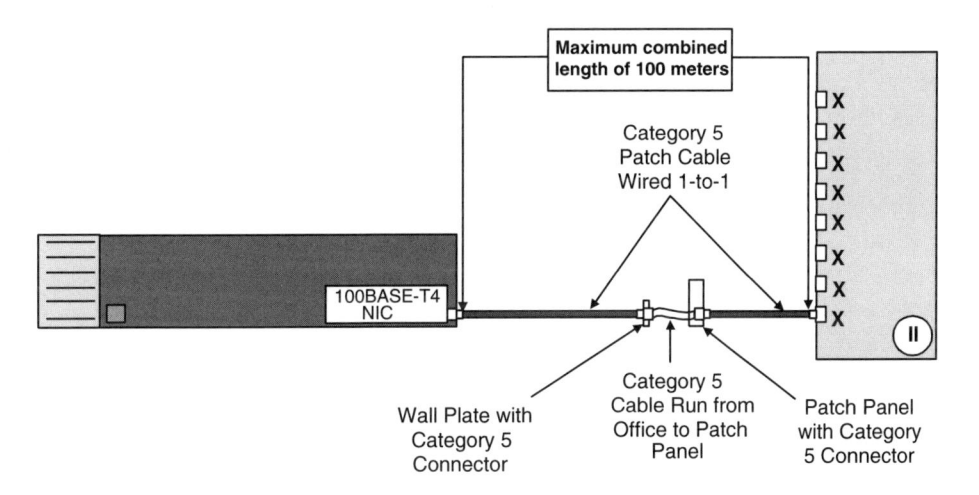

**Figure 6.3:** Simplified 100BASE-T4 connection to a repeater

To meet the CAT3 or CAT5 specifications requires more than just using CAT3 or CAT5 cabling. The connectors that terminate the cables and are used in the wall plates and patch panels must all meet CAT3 or CAT5 specifications to be effective.

The plug ends used to terminate the CAT3 or CAT5 cabling are 8-pin RJ-45 style connectors. The four pairs of wires required for 100BASE-T4 use all eight of the pins of the connector (see Fig. 6.4).

The transmit and receive signals are now polarized by the positive signal carried on one of the wire pairs and the positive signal carried on the other.

*CHAPTER 6*                                    *100BASE-T2, T4, and TX*

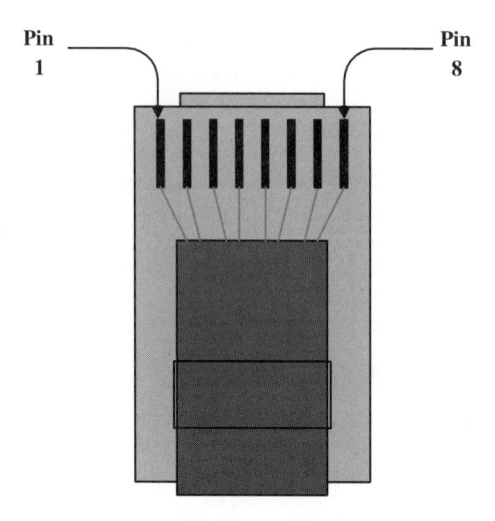

**Figure 6.4:** RJ-45 connector

## 6.7 100BASE-T4 Pin Assignments

1—TX_D1+

2—TX_D1-

3—RX_D2+

4—BI_D3+

5—BI_D3-

6—RX_D2-

7—BI_D4+

8—BI_D4-

# 6.8 100BASE-T4 Crossover

1—3
2—6
3—1
6—2
4—7
5—8
7—4
8—5

The pin out for 100BASE-T4 is exactly the same for the two pairs of wires used in 10BASE-T, 100BASE-T2, and 100BASE-TX. So if the cables meet the CAT5 specifications, they can be used for many purposes.

## 6.8.1 100BASE-T4 Repeaters

There are two types of repeaters defined for use with 100BASE-T4: Class I and Class II. The repeaters must be labeled with either a I or II centered in a circle to indicate the class of the repeater.

### *Class I Repeater*

The Class I repeater translates the incoming signals to digital form and then retranslates them to line signals as they are sent back out. 100BASE-TX, 100BASE-T2, 100BASE T4, and 100BASE-FX segments, which use different signaling techniques, are connected. Only one Class I repeater should be used per collision domain.

### *Class II Repeater*

Class II repeaters are limited to repeating only like signals. This means that only 100BASE-T4 segments would appear on a single Class II router. This restriction results in smaller timing delays. The smaller timing delay means that a maximum of two Class II repeaters can be used in a given collision domain.

### 6.8.2  100BASE-T4 Link Integrity Check

The transceiver (PHY) circuitry monitors the receive data path for activity to determine if the link is operational. When there are no stations transmitting the 100BASE-T4, PHY transmits link pulses to assure link integrity. Called Fast Link Pulses, these signals are used in conjunction with the auto-negotiation mechanism, allowing hubs that permit connection of both 10Mbps and 100Mbs to detect the speed of the link.

## 6.9  100BASE-TX

The 100BASE-TX standards major components are the media and the Physical Layer (PHY), or transceiver, and repeaters.

It is interesting to note that the 100BASE-TX leverages the Fiber Distributed Data Interface (FDDI) physical media standards.

## 6.9.1 100BASE-TX Media

The 100BASE-TX standards support the use of either Category 5 (CAT5) UTP or 150W STP cable. Two pairs are used: one pair for transmitting data (TX) and one pair for receiving data (RX).

The maximum length of CAT5 cable is 100 meters. Unlike 10BASE-T, where the maximum length is determined by signal strength, 100BASE-TX is limited by round-trip timing specifications. This means that unlike 10BASE-T, which permits lengths to be extended as long as the signal quality continues to meet the specifications, 100BASE-TX has an absolute maximum of 100 meters. This length includes the cable used to connect the network device (computer for example) to the wall plate, the wall plate to the cross connect panel, and the cross connect panel to the repeater (see Fig. 6.5).

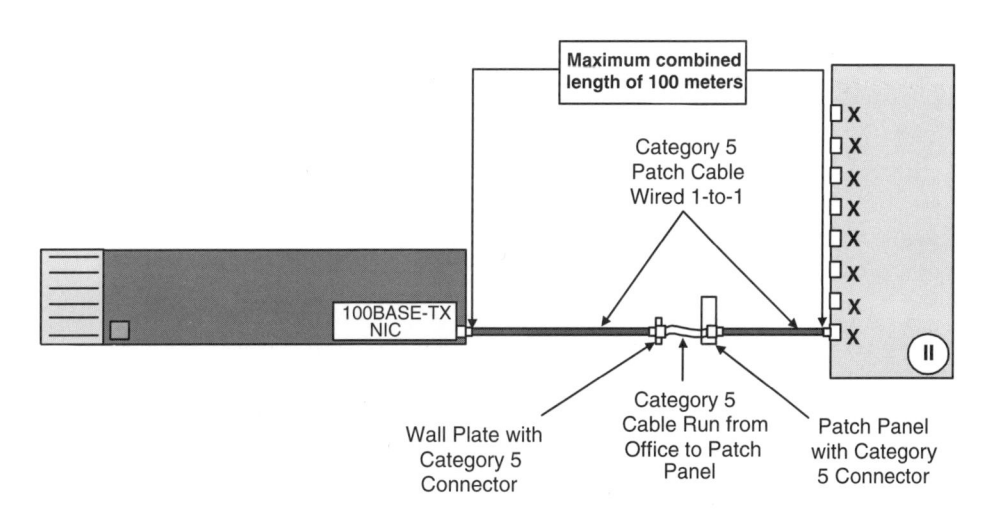

**Figure 6.5:** Simplified 100BASE-TX connection to a repeater

*CHAPTER 6* *100BASE-T2, T4, and TX*

To meet the CAT5 specifications requires more than just using CAT5 cabling. The connectors that terminate the cables and are used in the wall plates and patch panels must all meet CAT5 specifications.

The plug ends used to terminate the CAT5 cabling are 8-pin RJ-45 style connectors. The two pairs of wires required for 100BASE-TX leave four of the eight pairs of the connectors unused. However, all four of the pairs should be connected. Connecting all four pairs of the cable provides the ability to use a different technology later, like 100BASE-T4, without having to replace the cable ends. In the event that a crossover cable is required it is recommended that the cable be wired as a 100BASE-T4 crossover. The two pairs required for 100BASE-TX are wired exactly the same for 100BASE-T4. The only difference is that the connection of the unused two pairs of wires are now configured properly for 100BASE-T4 (see Fig. 6.6).

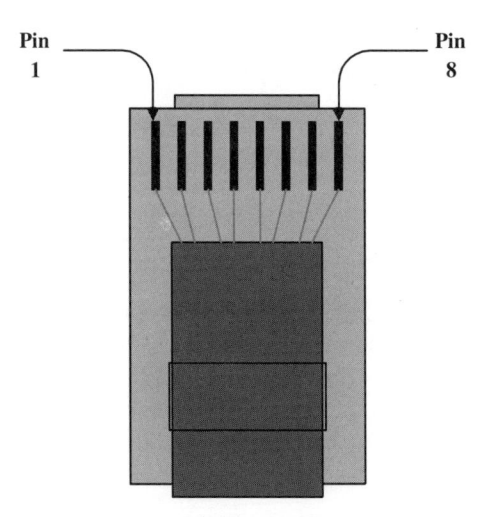

**Figure 6.6:** RJ-45 connector

The transmit and receive signals are now polarized by the positive signal carried on one of the wire pairs and the positive signal carried on the other.

## 6.10 100BASE-TX Pin Assignments

1—TD+
2—TD-
3—RD+
4—Not Used
5—Not Used
6—RD-
7—Not Used
8—Not Used

## 6.11 100BASE-TX Crossover

1—3
2—6
3—1
6—2

The pin out for 10BASE-T is exactly the same as 100BASE-TX. So if there are 10BASE-T line cords or patch cords available that meet the CAT5 specifications, they can be used.

### 6.11.1 100BASE-TX Repeaters

There are two types of repeaters defined for use with 100BASE-TX: Class I and Class II. The repeaters must be labeled with either a I or II centered in a circle to indicate the class of the repeater.

*Class I Repeater*

The Class I repeater translates the incoming signals to digital form and the retranslates them to line signals as they are sent back out. 100BASE-TX, 100BASE-T2, 100BASE T4, and 100BASE-FX segments, which use different signaling techniques, are connected. Only one Class I repeater should be used per collision domain.

*Class II Repeater*

Class II repeaters are limited to repeating only like signals. This means that only 100BASE-TX segments would appear on a single Class II router. This restriction results in smaller timing delays. The smaller timing delay means that a maximum of two Class II repeaters can be used in a given collision domain.

### 6.11.2 100BASE-TX Link Integrity Check

The FDDI signaling technique, on which the 100BASE-TX signaling is based, sends signals continuously, even when there are no stations that are attempting to transmit data. The activity of constantly receiving data should be enough to ensure that the link is operational.

However, the 100BASE-TX transceivers, which use the 8-pin RJ-45 style connectors, also transmit link pulses. Called Fast Link Pulses, these signals are used in conjunction with the auto-negotiation mechanism, allowing hubs that permit connection of both 10Mbps and 100Mbs to detect the speed of the link.

## 6.12 Chapter 6 Review Questions

1. What is a significant difference between clause 23 and clause 24?

2. What are two unique things found in the 100BASE-T4 specification?

3. What physical hardware does the MAC correspond to?

# Chapter 7

# 100BASE-FX

## 7.1 Introduction

Fast Ethernet is not constrained to run on shielded or unshielded twisted pair cabling; it can also run on fiber optic cabling.

## 7.2 100BASE-FX

The 100BASE-FX standards major components are the media and the Physical Layer (PHY), or transceiver, and repeaters.

### 7.2.1 100BASE-FX Media

Fiber optic cable uses pulses of light instead of electronic signals to transmit data. Fiber optic cables can be used for either baseband or broadband applications. Baseband applications have a single channel. Broadband applications have multiple channels. Each channel can be used as a separate network segment.

The number and size of the fibers vary from cable to cable. However, the standard fiber cable has a fiber core of 62.5 microns and a 125-micron sheath (62.5/125). The number of fibers in the sheath may vary.

The maximum permitted length of fiber optic cable is 412 meters. 100BASE-FX is limited by round-trip timing specifications. This means that 100BASE-FX has an absolute maximum of 412 meters. This length includes the cable used to connect the network device (computer for example) to the wall plate, the wall plate to the cross connect panel, and the cross connect panel to the repeater.

## 7.2.2 100BASE-FX Repeaters

There are two types of repeaters defined for use with 100BASE-FX: Class I and Class II. The repeaters must be labeled with either a I or II centered in a circle to indicate the class of the repeater.

### *Class I Repeater*

The Class I repeater translates the incoming signals to digital form and the retranslates them to line signals as they are sent back out. 100BASE-TX, 100BASE-T2, 100BASE T4 and 100BASE-FX segments, which use different signaling techniques, are connected. Only one Class I repeater should be used per collision domain.

## *Class II Repeater*

Class II repeaters are limited to repeating only like signals. This means that only 100BASE-FX segments would appear on a single Class II router. This restriction results in smaller timing delays. The smaller timing delay means that a maximum of two Class II repeaters can be used in a given collision domain.

### 7.2.3 100BASE-FX Link Integrity Check

The transceiver (PHY) circuitry monitors the receive data path for activity to determine if the link is operational.

# Chapter 8

# Media

## 8.1 Introduction

Ethernet and Fast Ethernet can be implemented using a variety of media. Each type of medium has its own benefits and liabilities. The most common types of media for 10Mbps Ethernet are AUI, thick coax, thin coax, unshielded twisted pair (UTP), and fiber optic cable. The most common types of media for Fast Ethernet are UTP and fiber optic cable.

## 8.2 AUI

The AUI cable is probably the most commonly used cable in 10Mbps Ethernet. This cable is most often used to attach devices, such as workstations, to transceivers. Commonly called a drop cable, the official name for the AUI cable is the Attachment Unit Interface.

CHAPTER 8　　　　　　　　　　　　　　　　　　　　　　　　　　　　*Media*

The four twisted pairs of wire contained in the AUI cable tend to make it a little stiff and cumbersome to work with. The AUI cable is terminated at both ends with connectors called D-Connectors, each having 15 pins. This connection is often referred to as a DIX connection, an acronym made from the three companies responsible for the development of Ethernet version 2—Digital, Intel, and Xerox. The male end of the cable connects to the equipment and the female end connects to the transceiver (see Fig. 8.1).

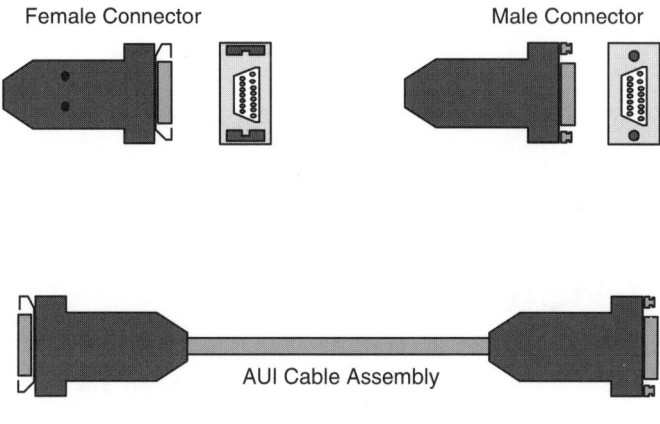

**Figure 8.1:** AUI cable and connectors

The female connector of the AUI cable has a slide latch assembly that is used to secure the connector to the transceiver. The slide latch assembly is also found on the equipment. These slide latch assemblies are marginal at best and are made from a soft metal that bends very easily, providing an excellent source for network headaches. The

## 8.2 AUI

majority of your problems will be eliminated if you take your time when making these connections and then make sure the cables are not stressed so as to pull on the connectors.

Common applications for the AUI cable include the connection of a workstation, repeater, or some other network device to a transceiver. One of the most common uses of this cable is to connect a workstation to a backbone cable via a transceiver (see Fig. 8.2).

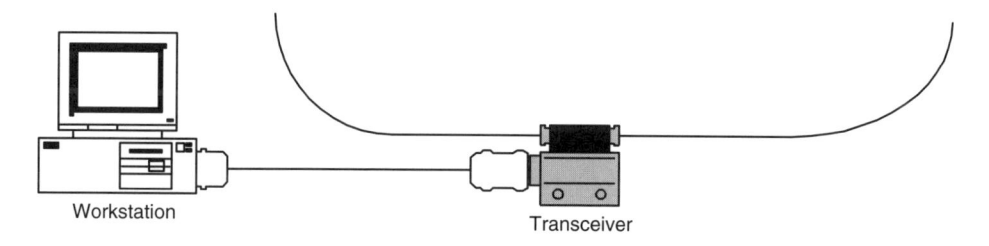

**Figure 8.2:** AUI connection of workstation to transceiver

Another common application for the AUI cable allows the workstation, or piece of networking hardware, to connect to a networking media that the equipment does not directly support. Because the DIX connector is very prevalent, most network cards and hardware are equipped with one. There are now transceivers with every type of common connection and an AUI connection.

Unlike all of the other media that will be discussed, the AUI cable is generally bought as an assembled unit. The maximum cable length for the AUI cable is 50 meters, or about 165 feet.

CHAPTER 8                                                                    *Media*

## 8.3 Thick Coax (10BASE5)

Thick coax was the original cable specified in the Ethernet version specification and is thus the most often used as a network backbone. The network backbone is what it sounds like, the spine to which the network connects. All of the hardware is interconnected through the common backbone cable (see Fig. 8.3).

The thick coax cable consists of a single copper center conductor covered with a dielectric material, which in turn is covered by two foils and two braids of copper wire. All of this is contained in a polyvinyl chloride (PVC) or Teflon type jacket. The Teflon jacket is used in applications requiring smoke reducing cabling. This cable is thick and, as a result, a little difficult to work with at times. This cable is marked with a stripe every 2.5 meters for tap attachment. The cable is terminated at either end with N-type connectors. At each of the terminating ends of the cable, a 50-ohm terminator is required.

To get from the thick coax to the network, a device called a *noninvasive tap* or *vampire tap* is required, or the cable can be severed and what is called an inline or invasive tap can be installed. These taps should be installed only on the stripes provided on the cable jacket. A transceiver is attached to the tap and an AUI cable is then attached to the transceiver to connect the node.

The maximum cable length for thick coax is 500 meters or 1640 feet. The maximum number of transceivers per segment is 100. The transceivers should be spaced on a multiple of 2.5 meters.

While thick coax was recognized in the EIA/TIA-568-A cabling specification, it was recommended against and it is anticipated that it will be removed from future specifications.[6]

---

6   TIA/EIA-568-A October 1995 Revision, Commercial Building Telecommunications Cabling Standard. p. 19, section 4.4.

**Figure 8.3:** Thick coax backbone

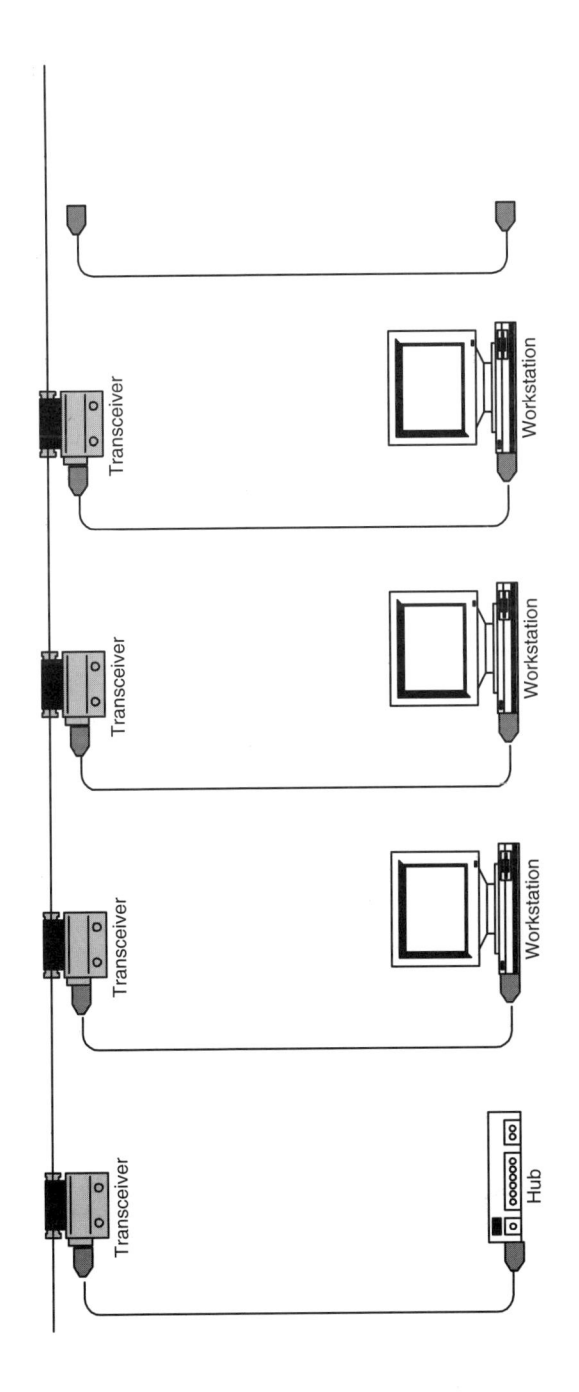

## 8.4 Fiber Optic (10BASE-F, 100BASE-FX)

Fiber optic cabling offers several significant benefits. Unlike the other media discussed, fiber optic cable uses pulses of light instead of electronic signals to transmit data. This results in a media that is impervious to RFI and EMI noise.

Fiber optic cables can be used for either baseband or broadband applications. Baseband applications have a single channel. Broadband applications have multiple channels. Each channel can be used as a separate network segment.

The number and size of the fibers vary from cable to cable. However, the standard fiber cable is multimode with a fiber core of 62.5 microns and a 125-micron sheath (62.5/125). The number of fibers in the sheath may vary, although two is the minimum. Select a cable with enough fibers to connect what you need plus an extra couple of fibers for expansion and repair. The fiber should comply with the ANSI/EIA/TIA-492-AAAA specifications.

The most notable liability of fiber optic cable is the cost to terminate. In recent years, some manufacturers have responded to this opportunity by producing less expensive and easier to operate termination tools. The expense of termination is found not only in the cost of equipment and connectors, but also in labor. Each connection should be polished and inspected before the connector is attached. Some of the new equipment helps to reduce some of this time-consuming process.

*8.5 Thin Coax (10BASE2)*

Fiber optic cable must be handled and installed carefully to avoid damaging the optic fibers. For Ethernet applications, the distance that can be spanned by fiber-optic cable is up to 2000 meters. However, it should be noted that the ANSI/EIA/TIA-586-A specifications require that if used for horizontal wiring, the maximum run should be less than 90m (295 feet).[7] Horizontal wiring is the portion of the network cabling system that extends from the work area network outlet, or connector, to the horizontal cross connect in the wiring closet. It includes the horizontal cables and patch cord in the wiring closet. The cabling is said to be horizontal because it normally runs horizontal along the floors or ceilings of the buildings.

# 8.5 Thin Coax (10BASE2)

Thin coax applications are commonly called thinnet or cheapernet. These versions use a 50-ohm coaxial cable. Thin coax cables are flexible and easy to handle. These cables are terminated with BNC connectors. The process of attaching BNC connectors is relatively easy.

The major liability of thin coax is its length limitations and ability to cause network disruption at every node. The maximum segment is 185 meters. Thin coax also allows for only 30 transceiver connections per segment.

The makeup of the coax cable is important. It is recommended to use a coax cable with a stranded center conductor. The stranded cen-

---

[7] TIA/EIA-568-A October 1995 Revision, Commercial Building Telecommunications Cabling Standard. p. 79, section 12.2.1.

ter conductor will result in a cable that is more resilient when flexed. The braid is also important, as the higher the percentage of braid coverage, the better the resistance to external noise induction.

It is very important to select either RG58/AU, the Belden 9907, or equivalent cable and use the selected cable exclusively throughout the installation. The reason is that while both of these cables meet the requirements for the media, they will have some nominal impedance differences. It is also extremely important to make sure that coaxial cable of a different nominal impedance, such as 75 or 90 ohms, which are both popular impedances, are not introduced into the network. The differing impedances will result in the signal traveling down that path in order to have some partial reflection. Signal reflection is when part of the signal actually bounces back toward the source. These reflections can be the base for a myriad of problems that are difficult to troubleshoot. Typically, the Beldon 9907, or equivalent, is the best (yet more expensive) cable of the two choices.

The selection of this cable for new horizontal cabling should be discouraged. While it was recognized in the EIA/TIA-568-A cabling specification, it was recommended against and it is anticipated that it will be removed from future specifications.[8]

---

[8]  TIA/EIA-568-A October 1995 Revision, Commercial Building Telecommunications Cabling Standard. p. 19, section 4.4.

## 8.6 Unshielded Twisted Pair (UTP) (IEEE 10BASE-T, 100BASE-TX, 100BASE-T2, 100BASE-T4)

The use of UTP for 10 and 100Mbps transmission is very popular. According to the IEEE 802.3-1996 specification, the design objective for use of UTP was 100 meters. However, longer lengths are permitted for 10BASE-T. This means that the maximum distances supported will be dependent on the cable specifications and the manufacturer selected, again for 10BASE-T only.

The specifications to adhere to for success are the EIA/TIA-568-A. In these specifications the UTP is well defined for the purposes of transmitting data at specific speeds. There is a detailed breakdown of the three main cable categories defined in this specification in Appendix A.

UTP provides the least expensive medium to install. The cost per foot and labor to install and terminate are lower than all of the other media. Even the connectors cost less. However, more cable is used; thus more labor is required, and more connectors are required. All of the additional cable, labor, and connectors typically result in a higher overall cost.

There was a big deal made of the fact that existing phone cabling can be used for the wiring. The use of existing phone cabling should be given careful consideration. Before the cable is used, it should be thoroughly tested to make sure that it will meet the quality requirements for the LAN. This testing can be accomplished using a hand-held tester. Another major consideration is that the existing phone cabling will be Category 3 at best. Category 5 rated cable may be a better choice for future implementations. (See Appendix B for cable category definitions and explanations.)

Take caution when considering UTP. While there are many excellent applications for it, there are also many pitfalls. Length considerations are the biggest pitfall to keep in mind. Again, the allowed length will be determined by the cable specifications and the manufacturer of the supporting equipment. If you purchase equipment that will drive a segment 150 meters, for example, and later want to switch manufacturers, you may find that you have nowhere to turn.

In the world of UTP, the quality of a cable is mainly defined by the gauge, number of twists, and consistency of twists. There is a method for grading cables called categories. The three main ratings are categories 3, 4, and 5. Category 3 cable is rated for 16MHz and is a fine choice for 10BASE-T and an adequate choice for 100BASE-T4 and 100BASE-T2. Category 4 is rated for 20MHz and is not widely used. Category 5 is rated for 100MHz, is required for 100BASE-TX, and recommended for 100BASE-T2 and 100BASE-T4 but not required for 100BASE-T2 and 100BASE-T4. All three categories are defined as having a 100-ohm impedance. Some UTP has 120-ohm characteristic impedance. Never mix cables of different impedance. The result will be unwanted signal reflections that appear as bad packets, which will in turn result in degraded performance.

# 8.7 Chapter Summary

There are basically two media types that are commonly used for new Ethernet networks—Unshielded Twisted Pair (UTP) and fiber optic.

## 8.7.1 Major Concepts

The two coaxial media that were used for the 10BASE2 and 10BASE5 are not recommended for new installations. They are both planned for exclusion from the next TIA/EIA-568-A cabling specification. These two media are only appropriate for 10Mpbs applications. The three media available for the implementation of 100Mpbs Ethernet are UTP, STP, and fiber optic cable.

The UTP should conform to the standards specified in the next TIA/EIA-568-A cabling specification. All efforts should be made to insure that only 100-ohm cable is used and that no varying impedance cables are introduced into the LAN.

The fiber optic cables should be a multimode fiber with a 62.5-micron fiber core and a 125-micron outer cladding.

Wiring diagrams are available in Appendix C.

## 8.8 Chapter 8 Review Questions

1. What liability of the AUI cable makes it potentially unreliable?

2. What is the significance of the stripes on thick coax?

3. What is the difference between baseband and broadband?

4. Name one liability and two benefits of fiber optic cable.

5. What is the issue when a segment of RG58/AU and Beldon 9907 cables are connected together?

6. Name two advantages of UTP.

7. What is the speed rating for a Category 3, 4, and 5 UTP?

8. What Ethernet implementations can be done on Category 3 cable?

# Chapter 9

# Hardware

## 9.1 Introduction

Six main hardware components are used in Ethernet networks: transceivers, hubs (this category includes repeaters), bridges, switches, routers, and Network Interface Cards (NICs).

The hardware used in the construction of the LAN operates at different levels of the OSI model. As each new piece of hardware is introduced, you will see that it is logically built on the shoulders of the equipment below it.

## 9.2 Transceivers

The transceiver is the most common hardware element in an Ethernet network. This unit is used in all Ethernet implementations. In Fast Ethernet implementations it is called the PHY. For simplicity, the term transceiver will be used for both the Ethernet transceiver and the Fast Ethernet PHY.

Transceivers can be integrated into other hardware or they can be separate units. The transceivers that are separate from other hardware are typically packaged in a relatively small box, usually about 1" x 4" x 4". The transceiver allows an AUI cable to connect to another media such as thick or thin coax, or twisted pair. The transceiver provides the mechanism to transfer the signal from the coax to the AUI cable and vice versa. It also generates the Signal Quality Error (SQE) signal.

The transceiver's most common application is to run drop cables from a thick coax spine to individual systems; however, there are transceivers to connect an AUI cable to thin coax, twisted pair, and fiber as well (see Fig. 9.1).

## 9.3 Repeaters

The function of a repeater is very straightforward—to repeat an incoming signal. The basic repeater connects two or more segments of Ethernet. Any signal from either segment is received by the repeater and the signal is then reamplified, retimed, and retransmitted by the repeater to all the connected segments. The repeater also performs collision checking. The repeater is often referred to as a hub.

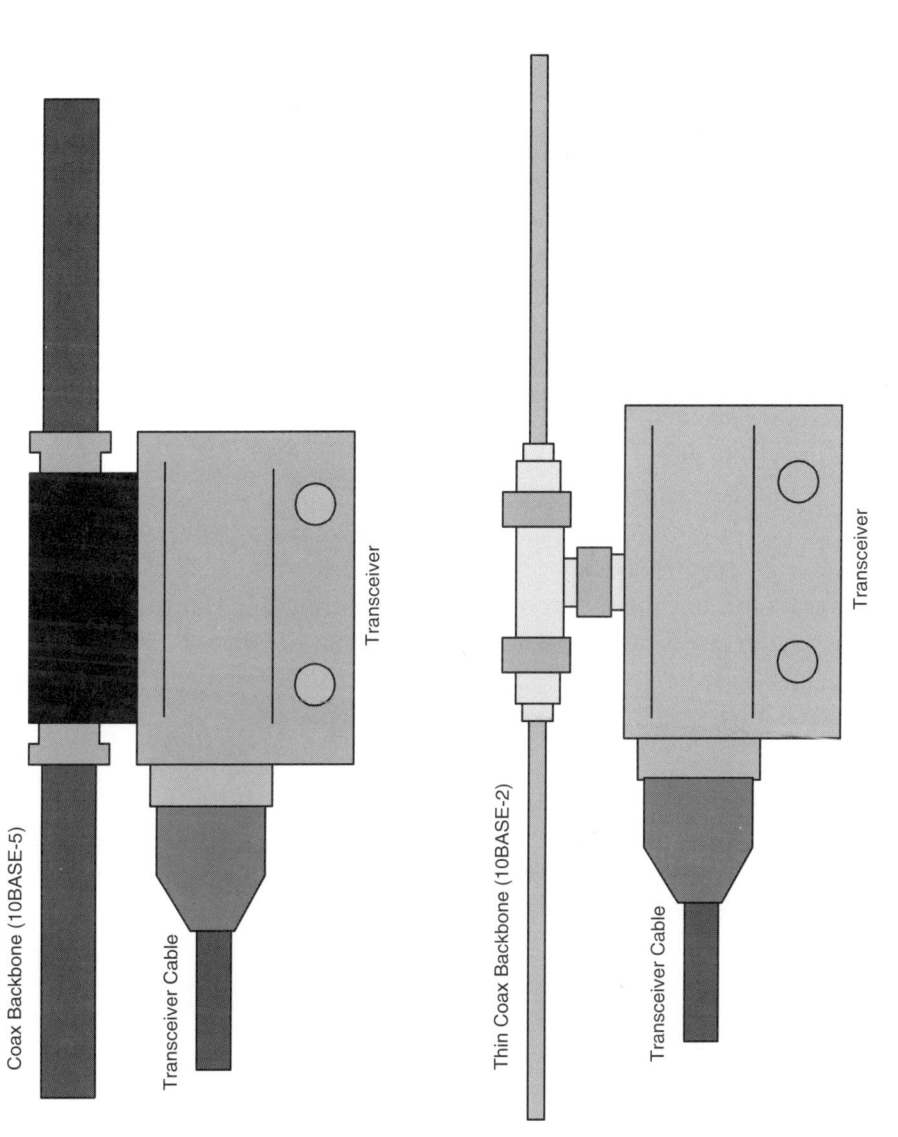

**Figure 9.1:** Transceivers

The repeater functions at Layer 1 of the OSI model. The Layer 1 functionality of the repeater allows the repeater to hear any transmissions and then reamplify, retime, and retransmit. The repeater also provides the functionality to detect collisions.

Through its function, a repeater allows the extension of a segment beyond the limitations of the single segment length rules. Take the following example:

- There is a system in excess of 150 meters away from a server to which it needs to be connected.
- The network is 100BASE-TX based.

In this example, we know that the length limitation of 100BASE-TX is 100 meters. Therefore, a cross-wired cable cannot simply be run between the two systems. However, if a repeater were placed so that neither segment were required to be in excess of 100 meters, they could be connected through the repeater (see Fig. 9.2).

Another function of the repeater is to provide simple connectivity to multiple devices. Take the following example:

- There are multiple systems that require connection to a server and a couple of networked printers.
- The network is 100BASE-TX based.

In this case, each of the system's network-based printers and the server connect directly to the repeater (see Fig. 9.3).

## 9.3 Repeaters

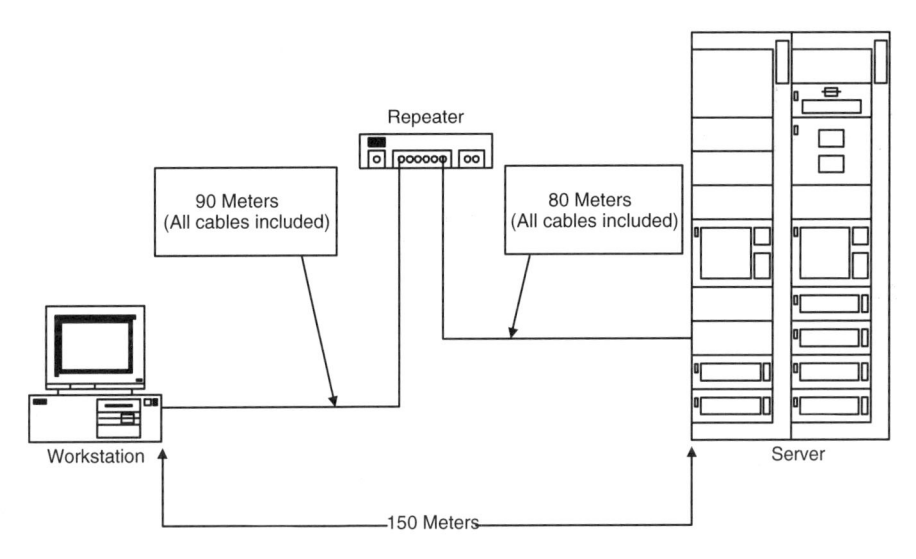

**Figure 9.2:** Diagram of example

This example demonstrates an application of a repeater used in a stand-alone situation. In a smaller application, say under 20 segments, a repeater might be used to provide all of the service. In this case, there is no backbone cable; each segment simply runs to the repeater.

The repeater is often used to connect systems and printers in an organized fashion. This application is best seen in the office environment where printers, systems, and other networkable devices are distributed across an office space—possibly multiple floors. In this situation, there are typically wiring closets that house the hubs, which in turn are connected via some form of backbone. The backbone might be coax, twisted pair, or fiber optic cabling (see Fig. 9.4 on page 113).

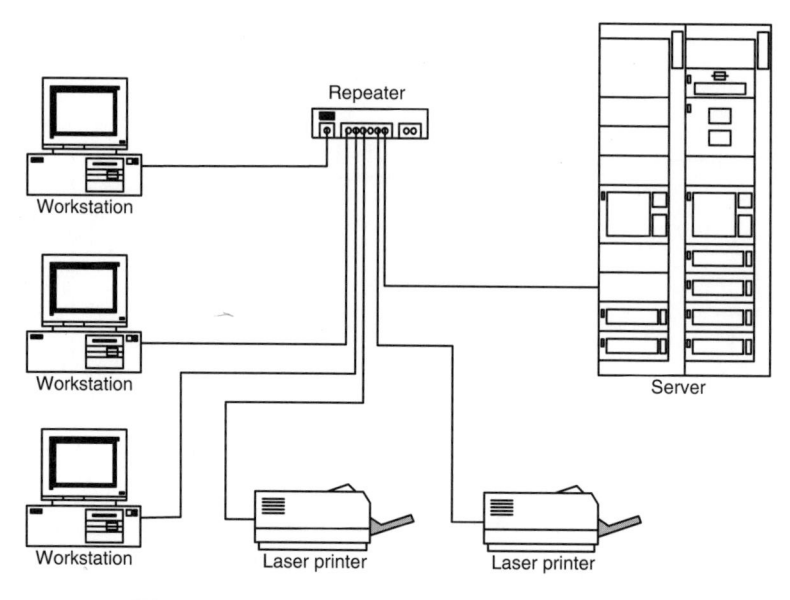

**Figure 9.3:** Diagram of second example

All of the segments connected together through repeaters are considered to be in a common collision domain. The collision domain is discussed in Appendix A. Simply stated, this means that all of the nodes attached to all of the segments in a single collision domain will detect a collision and respond to it.

The fact that the collision must be able to be detected by all of the nodes connected to all of the segments attached to the repeaters results in some rules that constrain the diameter (how many repeaters and how long the segments are that interconnect the repeaters) of the network.

*9.3 Repeaters*

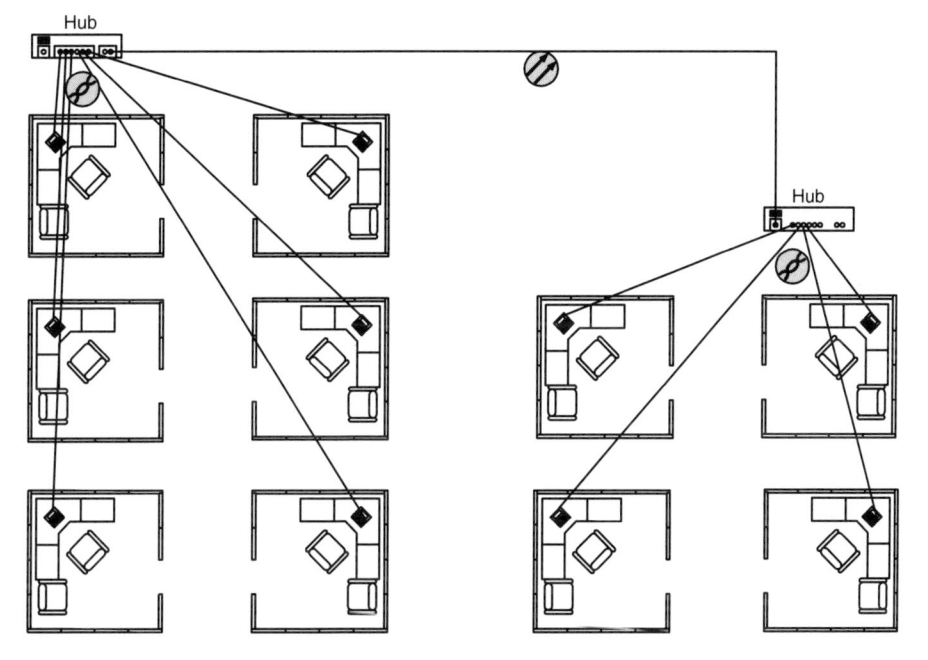

**Figure 9.4:** Simplified office layout with repeaters

## 9.3.1 10Mbps Ethernet Repeater Rules

In 10Mbps Ethernet networks the general rule is called the 5-4-3 rule for the construction of a one collision domain (see Fig. 9.5). This rule is broken out as follows:

- Five segments between stations maximum.
- Four repeater hops maximum.
- Three mixing (10BASE-F or Coax) segments max.

CHAPTER 9 　　　　　　　　　　　　　　　　　　　　　　　　　　Hardware

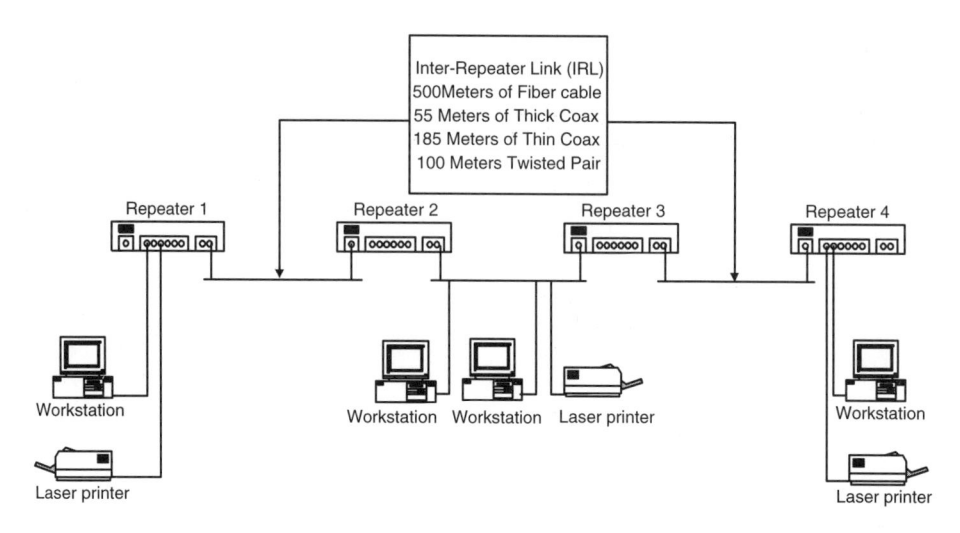

**Figure 9.5:** Simplified drawing of 5-4-3 rule

## 9.3.2 Fast Ethernet Repeater Rules

Fast Ethernet networks are also constrained to the same maximum diameter based on the same concept of round-trip collision delay which affects a 10Mbps Ethernet.

There are two types of repeaters defined: Class I and Class II. The repeaters must be labeled with either a I or II centered in a circle to indicate the class of the repeater.

## 9.3.3 Class I Repeater

The Class I repeater translates the incoming signals to digital form and then retranslates them to line signals as they are sent back out. This permits the repeater to have 100BASE-TX/FX and 100BASE-T2/T4 segments, which use different signaling techniques connected. Only one Class I repeater can be used per collision domain.

### 9.3.4 Class II Repeater

Class II repeaters are limited to repeating only like signals. This means that only 100BASE-TX and FX, 100BASE-T2, or 100BASE-T4 segments would appear on a single Class II router. This restriction results in smaller timing delays. The smaller timing delay means that a maximum of two Class II repeaters can be used in a given collision domain.

### 9.3.5 Repeater Summary

In summary, a repeater is simply a network device that connects two or more segments of Ethernet. Any signal from either segment is received by the repeater and the signal is then reamplified, retimed, and retransmitted by the repeater to all of the connected segments.

Repeaters take no logical action on transient frames. The repeater ignores the Ethernet packets. It only regenerates the incoming signals and retransmits them back out on all ports.

## 9.4 Bridges

Bridges are somewhat like repeaters in that they will allow two similar or dissimilar segments of a network to be joined together. However, the function of a bridge is different than the function of a repeater. The functional difference is that unlike the repeater, the bridge actually looks at each Ethernet packet that it receives. The bridge analyzes the destination field of the incoming packet and then determines how to handle the packet. The ability to determine the destination port for a given packet is based on the bridge's ability to capture the information about what addresses are communicating on each port. Using this information, the bridge is able to determine if the packet it is sensing on a given port should be ignored because the destination is on the LAN connected to that port or if it should pass the packet through to another port. Collisions are not passed through the bridge.

This function allows the bridge to isolate collision domains. Like the repeater, the segments on either side of the bridge are considered separate in terms of length rules. In other words, a bridge could be used in place of a repeater in the example given earlier, if the designer wanted to both extend the diameter of the network and create separate collision domains.

The following example should help illustrate the concepts of traffic isolation that have been discussed. Say nodes one through six are attached to network segment A and nodes seven through eleven are attached to segment B. Both segment A and segment B are considered to be the same subnet. In our example, the networking protocol uses a two-part logical address for each node. The first part is the subnet identification and the second part is the node identification for the given subnet. Referring to Fig. 9.6, the address for Node 1 on subnet A is A.1, indicating Node 1 of subnet A. The address for Node 7 attached to subnet A is A.7. Traffic generated by A.1 intended for A.2 will not be

## 9.4 Bridges

generated on segment A.2. However, traffic generated by A.1 intended for A.7 would transparently traverse the bridge, consequently causing the traffic to be seen on both sides of the bridge. If nodes A.1 and A.5 were to transmit simultaneously, the resulting collision would be seen only on segment A.1. The mechanism that allows this isolation is the functionality provided by Layer 2 of the OSI model.

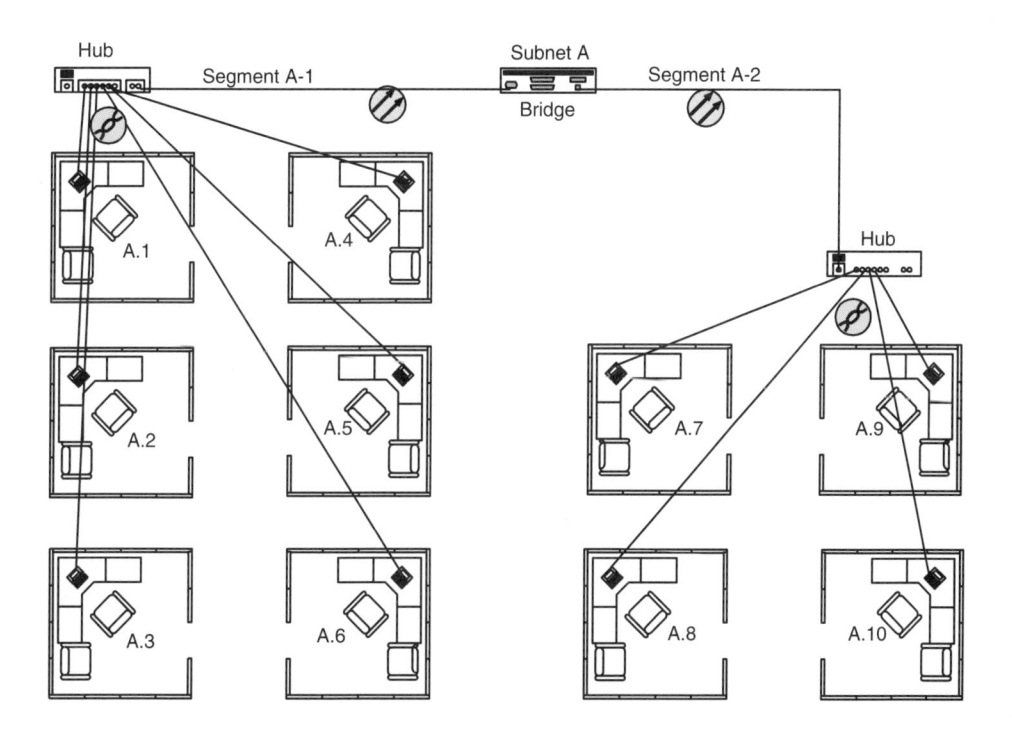

**Figure 9.6:** Simplified example of bridged subnetworks

If a network is sluggish because of an overload of network traffic, a bridge may be the answer. If you know that a group of nodes produces a heavy amount of traffic and those nodes are mostly communicating among themselves, then it may be best to install a bridge that would separate this group from the other nodes. The result would be that the users in the low usage group would experience an increase in network throughput. The other group would also experience an increase in network throughput, but depending on the amount of traffic they are producing, they may not notice the increased performance as much as the lower usage group.

The bridge can only help with traffic that is on the network. Performance problems caused by a server that is unable to handle the processing load, or applications that are poorly written for network use, cannot be solved with a bridge.

The network designer or administrator must understand the characteristics of the network in order to place the bridge at the proper point in the network and provide the maximum benefit. The ability to characterize the network traffic and functionality can be, and most often is, a very complex issue, which because of its scope will not be addressed in this book.

## 9.5 Switches

The switch behaves very much like a bridge. The switch is an active network device that analyzes the packets as they are received. Based on the destination address in the received Ethernet frame, the switch

## 9.5 Switches

then transfers that packet to the appropriate port. In effect, the switch temporarily switches the receiving port to the destination port based on the contents of the destination address field of the Ethernet frame. A temporary connection is created as there is a need. However, once the Ethernet frame has been transferred, the connection is switched off.

The Ethernet switch maintains a table associating physical ports with the Ethernet MAC addresses directly connected to the ports. Transfers between ports can occur in parallel.

There are three methods used to forward Ethernet frames through a switch. They are store-and-forward, cut-through, and modified cut-through.

### 9.5.1 Store-And-Forward

The store-and-forward method is used by bridges and can also be employed with switches. Using the store-and-forward method, the switch will store the complete incoming Ethernet frame in its internal buffers before sending it back out on the appropriate port.

### 9.5.2 Cut-Through

Using the cut-through method, the switch reads the Ethernet frame only up to the point where it is able to read the destination address. Once the destination address segment of the Ethernet frame is received, the switch creates the appropriate temporary connection and forwards the packet.

This method results in much lower latency time than the store-and-forward method. However, there is one significant drawback. The drawback is that because the switch examines the Ethernet frame for only the destination address, it has no way of determining if the packet is corrupted. The result is that if a packet is corrupted, the switch using this method will forward a corrupted packet.

### 9.5.3 Modified Cut-Through

The store-and-forward method does not forward corrupted packets but instead includes a significant latency while it stores the entire packet before forwarding it. The cut-through method provides a significant reduction in latency by examining the packet only until the destination address is known before creating the virtual connection. However, the cut-through method forwards corrupted packets. The modified cut-through method is an attempt to combine the best attributes of both the previous methods to provide low latency without forwarding corrupt packets.

To accomplish this, the modified cut-through method permits the switch to read the Ethernet frame through to the first 64 bytes of the packet. With the first 64 bytes read, the switch will most often be able to determine if a packet has been corrupted by a collision.

## 9.6 Routers

The router has the same OSI model Layers 1 and 2 functionality as the bridge, plus it is able to function at Layer 3 of the OSI model as well.

## 9.6 Routers

The OSI model Layer 3 functionality allows the router to make *decisions* on how to route packets that it receives. These decisions are based on parameters that are programmed into the router. The decisions that are programmed into the router are generally referred to as routes.

The concept of routing is relatively simple. The router is programmed with a set of rules. These rules tell the router where specific subnets are attached. For example, a router may have four Ethernet ports. A separate subnet would be attached to each of the ports. The router keeps a table of what subnets are connected to which port. As requests are made by nodes on one of the subnets to communicate with nodes on a different subnet, the router will forward the frames to the appropriate port.

Routers can also be programmed to perform based on a set of rules. In these cases, the router is programmed to determine what protocol may pass to or from its connected subnets. Take the following example. If a network administrator desired to allow only a specific network protocol type of packet called SMTP (Simple Mail Transfer Protocol) to cross from subnet A to subnet B, the administrator could program the router to permit only this protocol to be permitted to pass through the router and no other protocols. The administrator could just as well allow all types of traffic to pass from subnet B to subnet A.

Programming a router is a complex issue and will require the administrator to understand not only the physical structure of the network but also the protocols used and the issues involved in the control of network traffic.

## 9.7 Network Interface Card (NIC)

The network node is called the Data Terminal Equipment or DTE. The DTE contains the required hardware and software to perform the Media Access Control (MAC) functions to send and receive Ethernet frames in what is called the Ethernet or network interface.

The most common configuration for the network interface is a card that is inserted into some sort of bus on the device. When a network interface is installed in a PC, the card is inserted into one of the PC bus interface slots (such as an ISA or EISA type slot). When the network interface is installed in a printer, there is a special bus or connector on the printer for the network interface to attach to. As the most common means of providing the network interface is with a card, it has garnered the nickname of the Network Interface Card or NIC.

The network interface can also come in the form of a specialized converter. The best example of this is a device that connects to the parallel port of a printer on one side and provides an Ethernet connection on the other. The internal workings of this device convert the Ethernet frames into the appropriate signals for the parallel port on the printer and vice versa.

When considering the purchase of a NIC for your system or device, consider the bus options that are available on the given system. As Ethernet is 10Mbps and Fast Ethernet is 100Mbps, you will want to connect the NIC to a bus that matches the speed of the network as closely as possible.

Another consideration is buffering. Buffering allows the NIC to store frames as they arrive from the network. As the system is able to process the incoming frames from the NIC, the data is moved from the buffer to the system. Typically, the bus interface that the NIC is connected to is not as fast as the network. Buffering helps to smooth the effects of the mismatched speed.

## 9.8 Review Questions

1. At what layers of the OSI model does a repeater function?

2. Can you create separate collision domains using a repeater? If so, how? If not, why?

3. At what layers of the OSI model does a bridge operate?

4. What functionality sets the bridge apart from a repeater?

5. When would you choose a bridge instead of a repeater?

6. What device provides virtual connections?

7. What is a virtual connection?

8. What are the three packet routing methods used by switches?

9. What is the best packet routing method used by a switch? Why?

# Chapter 10

# Design

## 10.1 Introduction

The network designer is placed in a very precarious position. On one side are the expectations of users and management and on the other side are the hard realities of design restrictions, time requirements, and budgetary needs. It is the designer's job to discern the real needs and objectives, communicate back what the realities are, negotiate for a reasonable solution, and fulfill the mandates of management.

There is no place for designers who try to solve all of the networking requirements in the fastest, least expensive manner, with no thought given to the long-term consequences. However, there is not only a place but also a requirement for the bold, brave, meticulous, and innovative.

The bold designer communicates effectively and realistically to management, creating realistic expectations. The brave designer stands up to vendors, remaining unshakable by what "everyone else" is doing. The brave designer will take the time to understand the technologies available and how they relate to business requirements for the LAN. The meticulous designer checks and double-checks the design against the rules. The meticulous designer also documents everything. The innovative designer sees obstacles as opportunities, finding seemingly simple solutions in the face of the impossible. All four of these traits of successful designers consider both the short- and long-term ramifications of their designs. This consideration is given to business requirements based on management projections of growth, technology changes, business models, and other business-related drivers. The successful designer is aware of the technologies available. However, this designer is also aware that the proper choice is based on business objectives and not what vendors tout as the "future."

## 10.2 Three Basic Rules

Of the many things to consider while working through a design, there are three rules that will help to keep the designer out of serious trouble. These three rules are

- Keep it simple.
- Document everything.
- Stay within the rules.

## 10.2 Three Basic Rules

### 10.2.1 Keep It Simple

Complexity leads to nightmares. The simplicity of a design will shine in the form of manageability and maintainability. Three major thoughts encompassed in design simplicity are

- Keep the media type changes to a minimum.
- Allow for access to all hardware and cables without scuba gear, chain saws, or having a contortionist on staff.
- Minimize the number of nodes per segment.

The main concept is to think with the perspective of having to manage and maintain the network on a long-term basis.

### *Media Changes*

As a general rule of thumb, it is best to try to design the network with a minimum of media changes. It is not always possible or wise to use only a single media. As the designer, you will need to evaluate your individual requirements. Minimizing the media changes will result in a final network design that is easier and less expensive to manage and maintain. With each media type change comes increased installation and troubleshooting complexities. As media types change there are increased numbers of hardware connections and equipment necessary to handle the differences. Each of these connections and pieces of equipment provide additional complexity and points to potential problems.

CHAPTER 10 Design

## Hardware and Media Access

When designing your network, think with future vision. Plan on needing to get at the cables and hardware sometime in the future. There are many installations where the walls have to be damaged to get at existing cable or to install new cable. There are also installations where the person doing the troubleshooting requires a 30-foot ladder to reach the transceivers located in the rafters. Think as though you are going to be the one responsible for servicing all of the cable and hardware problems and expansions personally.

The biggest part of this process is in the planning; for example, planning to install conduit for the network cable that will be run inside the walls. This conduit would allow additions and deletions of cable in the walls to be done without causing any damage to the walls. The result is a dramatic increase in modification efficiency due to faster changes without requiring wall repairs. While you are thinking about the conduit, also plan on using a larger diameter than you need. For example, a half-inch diameter conduit may be all that is required to run a couple of twisted pair or thin coax cables, but maybe you should consider installing a one-inch diameter conduit, or even two one-inch diameter conduits. This extra space will allow new cables to be added easily.

## Minimize Number of Nodes

When designing a network with a topology that allows more than a single node per leg, like 10BASE2, it is often best to minimize the number of nodes per leg. The thought here is very simple. If there are 10 nodes on a leg and there is a problem with that leg, say the port on the hub

## 10.2 Three Basic Rules

fails, then there are 10 nodes affected by the problem. However, if there are only 6 nodes on that same leg, then there are only 6 nodes affected.

Also consider how many segments are connected to each hub. Hubs come in various sizes—4, 8, 48 ports, or more. If the hub fails, how many users are affected?

This is a balancing act between business needs and practical design. Spare equipment to provide spares for hubs needs to be part of this consideration.

## 10.2.2 Document Everything

There was an excellent electrical design engineer who, when asked about his design prowess, advised others to "Write it all down." When asked, "Who has time to write it down?" he responded, "Someone who does not have time to relearn." How does documenting failures and successes, thoughts and ideas, help make you a good designer? This documentation process helps to sort out and provide a reference back to thoughts and actions that have been part of a design. A major mistake that is often made is thinking that we will remember some idea or event. The harsh reality is that few people can remember the details of thoughts and actions effectively for extended periods of time. The concept of a design journal, in which the thoughts and activities involved in a design are recorded, is to be able to reflect back on the process of design.

The design journal explains the logic, long forgotten, of why one solution was selected over another. A comprehensive history of "what happened when…" can be captured. The journal comes to the rescue when management asks why some part of the design is done a certain way, and you are able to explain that the implementation methodology in question was to meet their expectations and requirements. This journal, created during the course of the design, will benefit the later stages of network life, installation, and maintenance.

During the installation phase, the design journal will provide answers to the sometimes difficult problems that often appear. For example, when an unforeseen obstacle blocks the path of a cable run, the journal will help to identify if there are available ports from another repeater to draw from and if the available repeater will provide the same connectivity as the original path. Time saved in making these decisions will help to keep the installation on track from both a time and budget perspective.

During the maintenance season of a network life, the design journal will provide a history of why the network is in its present configuration and will shine a light on ways to expand or change the topology of the network. For example, take a department that has both a company-wide LAN and a private LAN running into each of its offices. Say that this department decides to allow another department to connect to their private LAN. The design journal will detail how the LANs are kept separated and may offer excellent insights as to some of the options for connecting the disparate LANs, while not providing access to the private LAN anywhere else in the company.

The design journal should be a permanent bound, stitched binding notebook with graph paper and prenumbered pages. The permanent binding will prevent the unnoticed loss of pages. The graph paper provides both ruled lines to write on and assists in the drawing of diagrams. The prenumbered pages make referencing previously recorded thoughts or events easier. Each entry should be dated and no blank pages or spaces should be left in the journal between entries.

*10.2 Three Basic Rules*

The second major component of documentation is the network drawing. The design should have a detailed and clear network drawing that provides a logical representation of how the network will be connected. There should also be a drawing that provides a physical representation of the facilities, clearly showing cable paths and hardware locations.

## 10.2.3 Staying within the Rules

Don't let disaster be the story about your design. Beware of vendors and others that tell you "it's okay, I've seen lots of sites that run lines that long." Never invite disaster by compromising your design. A good design identifies the boundaries and works within them by a comfortable margin.

Some manufacturers design their equipment to perform beyond the normal Ethernet specifications. For example, some say they will allow you to run lines beyond the distances specified. The dilemma you are caught in is whether to include dependence on the extra capability of the manufacturer in your design or find another way around the problem.

To help make this decision, find out if any other major manufacturers offer the same capabilities. If they do, find out if their equipment is compatible with your selected manufacturers. Next, investigate the costs of working around the restriction that is causing you to consider breaking the rules. It is not in your best interest to design a network that is manufacturer specific. If the relationship with the manufacturer becomes strained, or if the manufacturer goes out of business and their products and support are no longer available, you want the ability to switch manufacturers and not have to replace any of the existing hardware, and/or redesign parts of the network.

## 10.3 Rules

The rules of length, numbers of nodes, and hardware usage will help to keep your design stable. Some rules exist because of a concept called a collision domain.

### 10.3.1 Lengths

As you will remember from Chapters 6 and 7, each different type of medium has a length restriction. It is best to try never to exceed 90 percent of the allotted length for any cable. By keeping cable runs at 90 percent of maximum length, there is a built-in margin of error provided. There will be times when you may need to run a cable to the very limit but try to avoid these instances. Weigh your options carefully; it is often best to spend a little extra on hardware. For example, increasing the number of ports on a multiport repeater may help avoid having a cable that is on the verge of being too long.

### 10.3.2 Number of Nodes

The total number of nodes per Ethernet network segment is restricted to a maximum of 1024. A segment is considered a complete network comprised of one or more legs, which can stand alone. While this is the theoretical limit, in practice, no single Ethernet network segment should have more than 200 nodes. Segments can be connected through repeaters, bridges, or routers to extend the geographical bounds of the network.

It is also wise to consider how many nodes per leg will be allowed. A leg is any length of medium that connects one or more nodes to a network. It is recommended to keep the number of nodes per leg to ten or less. However, the rules do permit more. The reasoning is that if there is a failure of the physical layer in one of the legs, then the number of nodes affected is minimal.

### 10.3.3. Hardware Rules

The most notable hardware rules have to do with repeaters. In 10Mbps Ethernet networks this concerns the 5-4-3 rule that is covered in detail in Chapter 9. With 100Mbps networks the repeater rules are different. Again, they are covered in detail in Chapter 9.

A hardware rule that is often overlooked is that if the network is to be CAT3 or CAT5 compliant, all of the network media and connectors must also be CAT3 or CAT5 compliant.

## 10.4 Design Step One

Step one in the design process is to identify the potential usage characteristics of the network. This step can be very tedious. However, it is important to understand the usage characteristics in order to have a clear idea of where extra bandwidth will be required. This identification will also provide understanding as to where areas with a high density of nodes in a single collision domain, at a lower bandwidth, would be acceptable.

To help get a clear picture of how the network will be used, there are two main methods that can be employed. The first, and most desirable, is to use tools that collect network characteristic information over a lengthy period of time. This information can then be put into report format and trends and usage requirements will be fairly obvious. Obviously, if there is no existing network, this is not feasible. However, it is feasible to characterize how the applications you use operate on networks with tools. Measurements may be available from other companies that have networks and have performed studies. Information may be available from users, groups, or software manufacturers as to who may have done these studies.

The second method is a manual method, where questions and observation provide insight from which to make decisions.

With either method the needs, goals, and desires of each of the groups that will be using the network must be well understood. The process of gaining this understanding will require interaction with people from each department that will be using the network. How are each of these groups using the network now? How do they expect the network utilization for their group to change over the next few months or years?

Often you will find that users and managers do not fully understand what they will use the network for. You will be the one who will offer suggestions as to what is available and how each function might be used. Once the users and managers understand the "what's" and "how's" of network usage, they should be able to provide some insights as to how much of the networking resources they might require.

One important factor to remember about all of the information you are attempting to collect is that it is not absolute. Answers are only going to be best estimates. Prompt those being questioned to answer the questions in terms of now, in the next year, and over the next five years.

## 10.4.1 Automated Method of Estimating Network Requirements

The use of tools to gather information about the network utilization characteristics is the preferred method. Tools come in many forms and are seldom inexpensive. Hardware and software monitoring tools should not be taken for granted. In many cases, these tools require specialized knowledge, training, or experience on the part of the user to be useful. Another consideration is that the collecting of data alone is insignificant. Knowing what data to collect and how to manipulate and present it is the difficult task. This will require a good understanding of the LAN, its operation fundamentals, and how it is utilized by business. Finally, the longer the period over which data is collected the better. This will assist in the discovery of usage trends that are driven by business cycles, such as the end of the month.

If there are no tools or expertise to use these tools properly, hiring a professional may be the best option.

## 10.4.2 Manual Method of Estimating Network Requirements

To help get a feel for how the network will be utilized, the following questions might be asked:

- Who in each group will use the network?
- How will each person use the network?
  - File transfers?
  - Printing?

- Data storage/retrieval?
- Communications (E-mail)?
- Terminal servers?
- File/application sharing?
- How often will each person use the network?
- For what duration will the use be?
- Will there be peak times of usage—daily, weekly, or monthly?
- Who will need to communicate with whom and by what means?

With these questions answered, you can start to ask the next set of questions.

- What size of files will be transferred and how often?
- What size of files will be printed and how often?
- How often and what size files will be printed to a postscript printer?
- How often and what size data files will be stored and retrieved from servers?
- Will the E-mail include many file attachments? What size will the attached files be? How often will they be transmitted?
- If terminal servers are to be put on the network, how much traffic do you expect them to generate? Traffic generation is a function of the server protocol and the usage level of the server. Some protocols, like LAT, are very efficient, others are not. No matter how efficient the protocol, you still need to weigh the usage level of the server.
- If files, applications, and/or databases are to be shared across the network, what is the activity estimated to be based on the size of files or the data structures and frequency of transmittal?

These questions help to quantify the usage and needs of the network by group and physical area. This will enable you to make decisions about segmentation, required hardware, and media types.

## 10.5 Design Step Two

Step two in the design process is one of the hardest. The difficulty of this process lies in the fact that we are most often dealing with estimations of how much, how long, and how often. The difficulty in obtaining absolute figures is inherent in how people perform their jobs. Files are opened at random times, documents are printed as required, and database queries cannot be timed. Even though this process of quantifying the information is difficult at best, it is a very important stage of your design.

### 10.5.1 Quantifying the Traffic Information

The first task is to try and make sense of the traffic information that you collected earlier. If the first step of collecting the data on usage characteristics employed the use of monitoring tools, then this step will produce more quantifiable information. The tools used to collect the data will also provide reports to quantify the traffic information.

When using a manual method to gather the network utilization characteristics, the information gathered does not provide hard quantifiable numbers that can be placed into formulas telling you what is really going on. The best that can be done is to get a "feel" for how the network will work with different types of traffic.

# CHAPTER 10 — Design

Without the use of monitoring tools, information about network behavior must be drawn from historical data gathered from existing network experience. If you presently have a network, try to identify any usage patterns that match those on your survey. If you do not have an existing network, try to talk with some other network managers and identify patterns on their networks that match those on your survey.

Another alternative would be to consult with the vendor that you are buying your networking products from. Try to find out what other customers have experienced with usages in your range and beyond. Putting blind trust in another network manager's advice could prove foolish. The same can be said with regard to vendors. This is not to say that all vendors are snakes, poised and ready to lie to us at the first opportunity. However, a little misinformation, intentional or not, will go a great distance in putting you in a very bad spot. If you are fortunate enough to have a network to survey, ask the following questions:

- How do the patterns that you are able to identify act in terms of network usage?
- Can you identify any types of processes on the network that cause a degradation of speed?

If you do have an existing network available to survey and are able to identify usage and patterns, you are very fortunate and well on your way to pulling it all together. What must be done now is to extrapolate from the given information performance parameters and issues facing the new network. The nodes that are going to create a traffic level that will cause the network to start to slow down have to be identified.

With a sense of what type of traffic problems, if any, are coming from where, and by what circumstances, you are ready to decide where to put in bridges and routers in order to isolate segments, reducing the traffic on each segment.

If you have no network to gather historical data from, or do not feel a great deal of confidence in your information sources, then you should consider hiring a consultant with experience in network design. The consultant should be able to help quantify your network loading and identify where, if at all, you will need to install bridges or routers. Interview several consultants. Ask the following questions to help you get a feel of their experience and abilities:

- How many networks have you designed that are of a like nature to mine?
- Who are your references? Local ones are of special interest.

It may be best to consider a consultant who has no products to sell other than their expertise. That way, inventories or pressure from manufacturers will not cloud the issues at hand. It is always in your best interest to call the references given and thoroughly check out the consultant.

## 10.6 Design Step Three

The work performed in the first two steps provides the critical information required to make decisions regarding network structure. The third step in the design process is to determine what the bandwidth requirements are for each of the network areas. This is where the network analysis tools have a definite advantage over the manual methods. The network tools will have provided the hard numbers that will allow for the creation of a reliable network.

After examining the utilization characteristics, decide where 10Mbps would be adequate and where 100Mbps would be well utilized. A common finding is that the segments connecting high-usage servers are good candidates for 100Mbps links.

## 10.7 Design Step Four

In step four, the goal is to identify where the networking equipment will be placed, any potential hazards that may exist, and the placement of each node.

First, you must have the layout of the facility. With the layout in hand, potential equipment closets are identified. Equipment closets should have adequate power, ventilation, and equipment. Access to the closet is also a consideration from both a security as well as an accessibility standpoint. Another consideration for equipment closets is centralization. The more centralized the closet, the shorter the cable runs.

The location of all electrical equipment with large transformers or motors, like industrial machinery, lighting, and any other hazards, should also be noted on the layout.

Again, with the layout in hand, determine each node's location and the location of all the areas to be wired for future growth. During the initial installation phase is generally a good time to place cable for

*10.8 Design Step Five*

future growth. The equipment to support the extra cable does not need to be purchased until those locations are ready to be activated. The advanced placement of cabling helps to minimize both the cost of the installation of those cables and the disruption to the normal work flow of your office. The costs are reduced in cases where contractors are used due to the fact that the labor force is already on site, so there are no reoccurring travel charges. Another cost savings is generated by the fact that the building is either torn up or not yet finished, so that the cabling is easier, resulting in lower labor costs.

## 10.8 Design Step Five

With the beginning and end points and the hazards identified in step three, you are now ready to determine the cable routes.

Locate the areas that will be the most suitable for the location of repeaters, bridges, routers, etc. These areas should have adequate ventilation to keep the equipment from overheating and should be readily accessible for servicing. Also make sure clean power is available for these locations.

It is advisable to not enclose any equipment, such as a transceiver, in a ceiling or crawl space. Equipment that is not readily accessible will be difficult to troubleshoot and/or repair.

Measure each run as accurately as possible. Allow a margin of at least 10 percent to cover slack. It would be wise to visit the site with the drawing and confirm that the route chosen for each run is realistic. Also review the lengths of each run. Look for obstacles, like beams

*CHAPTER 10* *Design*

or soffets, that will cause the length of the run to be extended. Make sure that each path is accessible after the company is fully operational. This may not always be possible, but it is highly desirable. Try to keep in mind that someone will eventually have to come back to service the cable at a later date.

Determine where multiple cables can be run at the same time. Significant cost savings can be had by running several cables. The cost reduction is generated by a reduced labor cost and potentially decreases the likelihood of "cable burn." Cable burn occurs when a cable is pulled across a stationary cable and the resulting friction causes the outer insulation of the fixed cable to be worn. This will cause many types of problems, the most troublesome being random shorts and cross talk.

Another consideration of the cable routes is future accessibility. This consideration involves future events such as new cable placement or cable repair.

When investigating the runs, make sure that there are no threats to the integrity of the cable. For example, do not plan to run cable through the supports for plumbing. As the building heats and cools, and as the earth shifts, the cable will become pinched between the pipe and its support and the cable will be severed or a short will be caused. Either of these problems will prove difficult to pinpoint. Identify where it would be good to put cable troughs and/or ladders. Cable troughs and ladders will help keep the cable out of harm's way and will provide a permanent supported path for the cable.

When the cable comes down from the ceiling, there should be either a plastic or metal conduit. The conduit may also be flexible or ridged.

## 10.8 Design Step Five

The main precaution when using metal conduit is to make sure that the edges, top and bottom, are not sharp. The conduit should be at least one-half inch larger than you need for the current cable plans. The larger the diameter, the easier to run cables now and add cables later. The conduit should run from three to six inches above the top plate to the top of the mud ring. The conduit will provide an efficient way to move or add cable to or from the location.

Design to keep the cable runs as short and as neat as possible. The less the cable has to go around, over, under, and/or through obstacles, such as plumbing and venting, the better. It would be wise to either have a good working knowledge of building codes that regulate how the cabling can be done or to hire a contractor who does.

As you plan your cable route, look for potential sources of RFI and EMI. Electrical lines and florescent light are two of the most common sources in the business area. Electric motors and heavy appliances are other sources. If you are not using a fiber-optic cable, try to keep a minimum of six inches from standard electrical sources. When you are forced to cross an electrical cable or conduit, try to cross at 90 degrees; this will minimize the noise induction to your cable.

As each cable route is charted, each cable run should be identified with a unique number sequence. This sequence can be alpha, numeric, or alphanumeric. This identification number should then follow the cable all the way back to the repeater, if one is used.

Finally, consider building movement. If your building is in an area that experiences earthquakes, make sure that your cable runs are free from potential damage that may be caused by building movement.

CHAPTER 10                                                                  *Design*

With your cable route figured out, the next step is to identify all of the points of connection. Each point of connection should be designed so as to avoid random grounding. This problem usually occurs with thin and thick coax and can be avoided by the use of rubber boots that cover the connections.

## 10.9 Design Step Six

Step six is to select the media that will be used to construct the network. Select the media based on the area where the media will be installed. Consider factors such as noise induction and accessibility to the cable.

### 10.9.1 Optical Fiber

You might select optical fiber cable for environments with high noise induction. Be careful to select proper racking accessories that will provide the proper radius of bend for the cable as it is terminated in equipment cabinets.

Optical fiber is often a good choice for a backbone cabling medium. It will provide the ability to upgrade to speeds greater than 100Mbps sooner than copper medium.

### 10.9.2 Twisted Pair

A twisted pair leg supports a single node only. Therefore, you will need to run a separate cable to each node location from the closet. Make sure that the data outlets for the equipment are placed so that the

*10.9 Design Step Six*

minimum length of cable will be required to run from the wall plate to the equipment. Whenever possible, use CAT5 cable. Even though the specifications may only call for CAT3, using the higher grade cable will provide for the ability to change the LAN implementation without having to replace the cabling infrastructure.

### 10.9.3 Thin Coax

Thin coax gives you the option of using Ethernet as it was originally intended to be used physically, in a bus topology. The cable can be run from the equipment closet and stitched through several offices before being terminated. Remember the rule of thumb: allow no more than 10 nodes per leg to minimize the impact if the integrity of a leg is compromised.

When selecting thin coax cable, select the medium carefully. Selection of a single type of 50-ohm cable, Belden 9907 or RG58/AU compatible, will provide the best resistance to external noise induction, offer less signal loss, and have fewer problems with reflections caused by mismatched impedance. The higher percentage braid coverage offered, the better resistance to external noise induction. Also, for thin coax, select a coax with a stranded center conductor instead of a solid center conductor. The stranded center conductor will be much more resilient as the cable is physically flexed than the solid center conductor.

### 10.9.4 Thick Coax

While it is not recommended for installation in new networks, a brief discussion of thick coax is included. Baseband coax is usually available from the manufacturer as "Ethernet cable." Normally, the cable is yellow or orange; the color is not important. It is striped every 2.5 meters. The stripe is important as it is the minimum distance for tap spacing. If you select thick coaxial cable for part of your network, think about how you will access the transceivers and taps at a later time for troubleshooting.

## 10.10 Design Step Seven

When selecting cable connectors, go first class. This does not necessarily mean to buy the most expensive connectors, but it does mean to buy the highest quality. Quality can be measured by the quality of the connection, the ease of assembly, and the robustness of the connector. Also make sure the connectors are a perfect match for the cable you choose. For example, when using a modular connector on a twisted pair cable, there are two types of modular connectors—those for solid conductors and those for stranded conductors. For the best results, use the appropriate connector.

There are a wide variety of methods for getting the same result with a connector. For example, BNC connectors for thin coax have two major methods of connector assembly.

One method consists of a center pin that is soldered in place and then the body is tightened on with a small set of wrenches, sometimes referred to as a "can wrench assembly." This method has proven to be a bit unreliable. Some people solder better than others. Some technicians

## 10.10 Design Step Seven

overtighten the assembly, causing damage, while some don't tighten the assembly enough, causing an unstable connection.

The other more popular method is the crimp style connector. With this method, the center pin is crimped to the center conductor and there is a sleeve piece that crimps onto the braid. Both of the connections provide a gas-tight connection when done properly. With the crimp style connectors, better tools will aid in making an almost foolproof connection every time.

After selecting the connectors, buy the proper tools. Tooling goes a long way in creating the success or failure of a connector. Again, the advice here is to buy the highest quality tools available. Tool quality is measured by the ease of use, the quality of its performance, and its robustness. A high-quality tool will help to assure a proper termination every time.

Before making a final decision on connectors, get a length of cable and use the selected tools and connectors to make a dozen or so connections. You should notice if the tools are easy to use and if the connections are tight, but not overly tight. Make sure that the connections look clean, no braid showing on the coax connectors. Also look to see if the connection process is fairly foolproof. For example, crimp tools that ratchet and do not release until the proper crimp has been applied are much more desirable than the nonratcheting ones. The crimp tool without the ratchet will provide a different amount of crimp each time it is used, providing an inconsistent connection quality. There is no totally foolproof tool, but there are many excellent choices available.

CHAPTER 10 　　　　　　　　　　　　　　　　　　　　　　　　　　　　Design

# 10.11  Design Step Eight

There are two stages involved with hardware selection. The first stage is to select the hardware type(s) required for the network. The second stage is to select an appropriate manufacturer.

## 10.11.1  Selecting the Hardware

The hardware selected will most likely be in service a minimum of three to five years and will represent a substantial sum of money. With these two factors in mind, remember to think toward the future. Consider equipment with growth potential that most closely matches your expected growth. For example, when the original network is installed, only 32 10Base-T ports are required. However, it appears that over the next two years, another 4 to 12 ports may be required. In this case, you want to make sure that the hub is capable of cost-effective expansion. Another example might be that currently all port requirements are 10Base-T, but it is expected that, at some time in the future, a fiber-optic line will be required for the manufacturing area.

Many manufacturers provide equipment with informative lights or displays. These lights and displays are more than nice to see. Many provide instant visual information. For example, lights that indicate proper power, heartbeat, collisions, errors, and proper termination can prove invaluable.

Equipment performance and reliability are critical factors. Often in the pursuit of performance, there is a great temptation to purchase equipment that is new to the market, often called the "bleeding edge" of technology. While not all of this bleeding edge technology is problematic, much of it is, and the title has been well earned. Most often, avoidance of this equipment is advisable for the first few months of its production and sale. The best advice given comes from a 20+ year sales veteran who stated, "let someone else work out the kinks." Get references from the manufacturer or sales representative. Call the references and get an evaluation from others who are using the equipment.

## 10.11.2 Selecting a Manufacturer

When selecting hardware, choose the manufacturer with the best track record in your type of application. For example, in the installation of a thin coax network, you might select manufacturer A because of their history of providing quality thin coax product. Manufacturer B may do a better job in twisted pair applications because of their focus on twisted pair technologies.

Look for a manufacturer that is stable, both financially and in product maturity. You want mature products, that is, products with a proven history. Try to avoid the "bleeding edge." Product maturity will help to provide a stable networking environment.

# 10.12 The Final Step

The last step in the design process is to double-check everything. Recheck the length of the cable runs, the hardware rules, and hazard locations.

The design process can prove very tedious with the checking and rechecking, and the efforts to quantify the usage information. However, if you are diligent and take the necessary time to give attention to each matter, your design will reward you in the installation and troubleshooting phases.

## 10.13 Chapter Summary

By this point you have now

- Identified the characteristics of the proposed network.
- Quantified the traffic information.
- Identified the bandwidth requirements.
- Identified the location of nodes, hazards, and equipment closets.
- Drawn the cable routes.
- Selected proper media types.
- Selected proper connectors and tools.
- Selected the proper hardware.

### 10.13.1 Major Concepts

Keep the design simple, minimize media changes, provide adequate access to media and hardware, and minimize the number of nodes on hubs or coax runs.

Document everything. This is tedious but necessary. Use a permanent bound, stitched binding notebook with graph paper and pre-numbered pages and stay within the rules.

The process of gathering the information necessary to properly design a LAN can be very tedious. At times, the process has to be

## 10.13 Chapter Summary

manual. In these cases, experience and detailed attention are the major design tools to be applied.

When using any automated tool for the collection of network utilization characteristics, gather data over an extended period of time. The minimum period should cover significant reoccurring events such as end-of-month reports. Automated tools require experience to operate in a manner that will provide usable information. If experience is not available in current staff, consider hiring a contractor with the experience and tools.

Identify the usage characteristics of the LAN. Where are areas that will permit a higher density of nodes? Where will the greatest bandwidth be required?

Carefully consider where equipment will be placed. Take into consideration accessibility, security, ventilation, environmental concerns, and electrical requirements.

Perform a walk-through of the facility to be cabled. Take detailed notes of the proposed cable paths. Consider using cable racks and conduits wherever possible. Take into consideration environmental threats to the cable or other obstacles to running the cables in the proposed path.

Make media selection based on all previous steps. Consideration for upgrades and environment should be given. Select high-quality connectors and tools to terminate cable ends.

Survey the marketplace, using magazines and peers, regarding equipment. Consider manufacturer's reputations, financial standing, focus in the market, and maturity of product line.

When all design steps are completed, double-check everything.

## 10.14 Case Study

A small manufacturing firm required assistance with the design and installation of a new LAN for their company. They would be moving from one facility to another and they wanted the new LAN in the new facility.

A meeting was set with the owner, the manager of Research and Development, and the operations manager to gather as much data as possible about the needs, desires, and goals of the company's network. After a brief meeting, the following facts had been gathered:

1. The company had 86 employees, all of whom used PC systems for conducting some part of their business.

2. The company had an existing 10BASE2 network.

3. There were two main servers: one dedicated to the mechanical design department and one for the whole company.

4. The resources to be shared were disks, printers, and a tape drive for network backups.

5. The company had hired a consulting firm to monitor the network over a three-month period and provide a detailed utilization report.

6. The existing LAN was configured per Fig. 10.1.

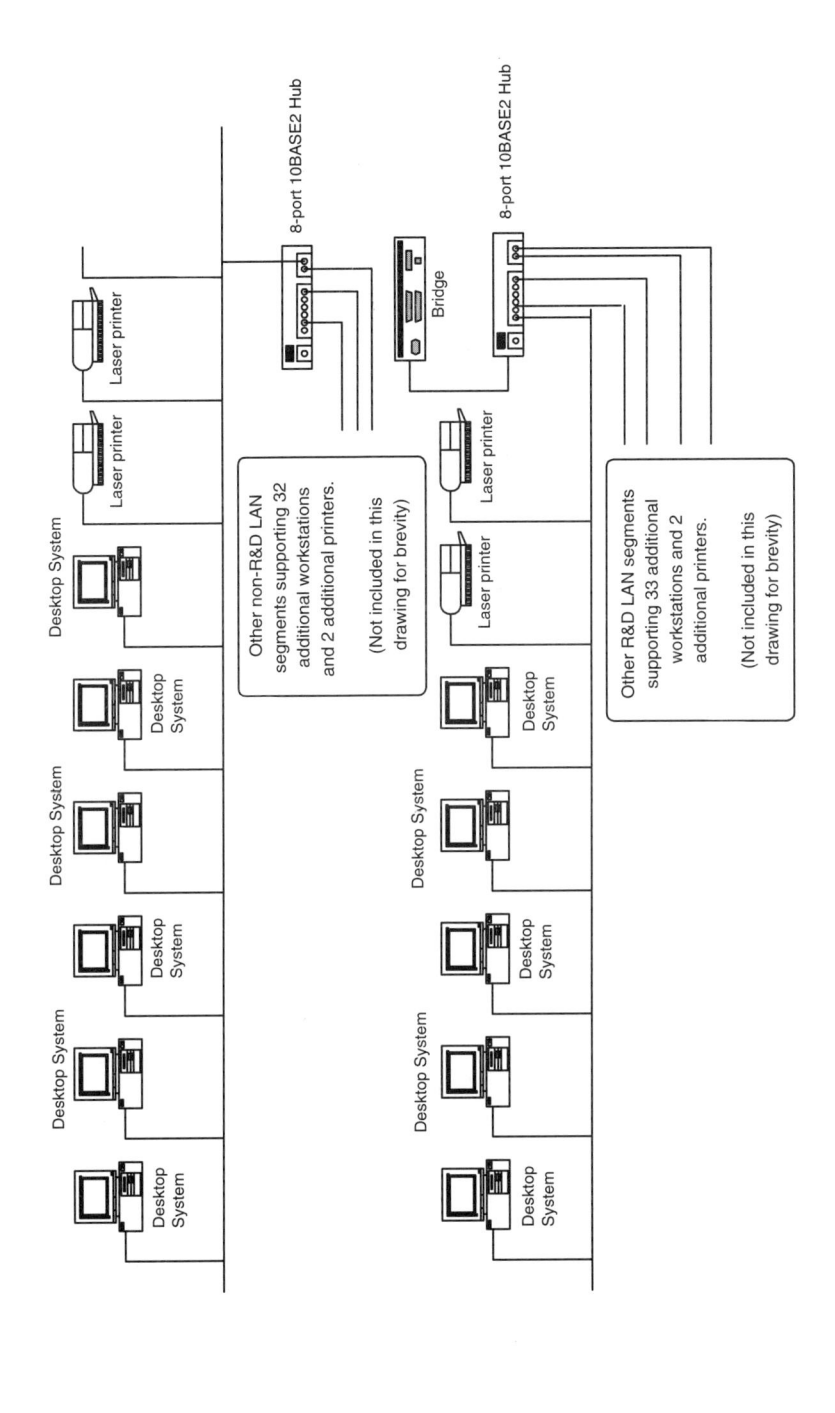

**Figure 10.1:** Logical network drawing of existing network

Further conversations with management revealed that there was a great deal of discontent with performance. All of the management employees stated that the management applications that resided on the server were less than responsive in the morning and especially at the end of the month. The Operations Manager stated that the accounting department wanted to be removed from the network because of application and printing problems that were at the worst at the month-end close. The R&D manager stated that users were starting to store critical drawings and engineering documentation on their local workstations instead of the server because of a lack of confidence in the network.

A review of the reports generated from three months of network monitoring revealed that the network had a significant bandwidth availability issue, which reached a critical crescendo at month end. During month end, the analysis of the traffic showed that the network was busy in excess of 80 percent of the time and over 25 percent of the traffic were either collisions or bad frames. During peak periods this could last up to two hours. The R&D LAN was dismal; the traffic analysis showed that the network was buried. The other LAN was in the same shape and the extra demand at month-end closing often caused the LAN to fail completely. That is, the traffic level was comprised of over 60 percent collisions for periods of five to ten minutes at a time.

Management was aware of the analysis and was able to see the congruency of the complaints and the network loading issues. They were also aware that major modifications might be required to rectify the current situation.

Further meetings with the R&D staff and review of detailed traffic analysis demonstrated that the staff relied heavily on a file server

## 10.14 Case Study

for engineering documentation and engineering drawings. The documentation transfers were fairly routine, small to medium file sizes of a few thousand bytes to a couple of megabytes. The drawings ranged from 1 or 2 to 20 plus megabytes. The documentation and drawings were to reside on the file server and be opened across the network for all to access, including creation and editing. A series of printers handled the output of the document and drawings.

The detailed review of the utilization characteristics of the networks demonstrated that the servers were adequate to the task during normal times, but during heavy transaction periods the servers were running at, or close to, capacity. Also, a review of the servers showed a lack of a disaster recovery plan in the event the servers experienced a catastrophic failure.

A breakdown of the usage statistics of the network demonstrated that users outside of R&D required an average of less than one-quarter of a megabit per second individual bandwidth for workstations over periods of 5 to 10 seconds, with the exception of the marketing group. There were individuals in the marketing group who routinely had bursts of 1 to 2 megabits per second for periods of up to 30 seconds. The combined usage of these users, 4 marketing and 34 others, would require around 16.5Mbps at peak to meet their needs.

This demonstrated that the bottleneck existed in two places—the LAN and the servers. Also evident was the requirement to increase the availability of the servers.

Management had agreed to add a server for R&D to split the load. One would be dedicated to the drawing files and processing and the other would be for documentation files and processing. A committee was also formed to investigate disaster recovery issues.

CHAPTER 10 _Design_

The analysis of the network usage patterns and plans resulted in the following network design proposal: use a small 100BASE-TX switch to which the two R&D servers and the business server would be connected. Use two 24-port 100BASE-TX hubs to serve the R&D users and the four marketing users. These two hubs would connect to the 100BASE-TX switch. Three 12-port 10BASE-T hubs would also attach to the 100BASE-TX switch to provide 10BASE-T connectivity to the users outside of R&D. Finally, a 12-port 10BASE-T hub would be used in R&D to connect the printer and another would be used outside R&D for the other printers (see Fig. 10.2).

With a set of build-out plans, a visit was made to the new facility for a physical inspection. The operations manager indicated where the computer room would be and where the equipment and cross connect panels would be placed. Notation on the site drawing was made indicating these locations.

In a survey of the site, two major obstacles were found. The first was an air conditioning duct that cut off the main path to the new computer room. The second was a fire wall that separated four offices from the rest of the building. The air conditioning duct was not on the plans.

During the survey measurements, the lengths of each run were taken and the site drawing was updated to indicate the distances. A strategy to go around the air conditioning ducts in the main path was mapped out. Notation on the site map was made to indicate where a small hole would be cut in the fire wall to place two three-inch diameter pipes for the cables. The modification would later be patched to meet local fire code restrictions and the extra room in the pipes would permit easy insertion of additional cables. Finally, the location of the cable racks was noted on the site drawing.

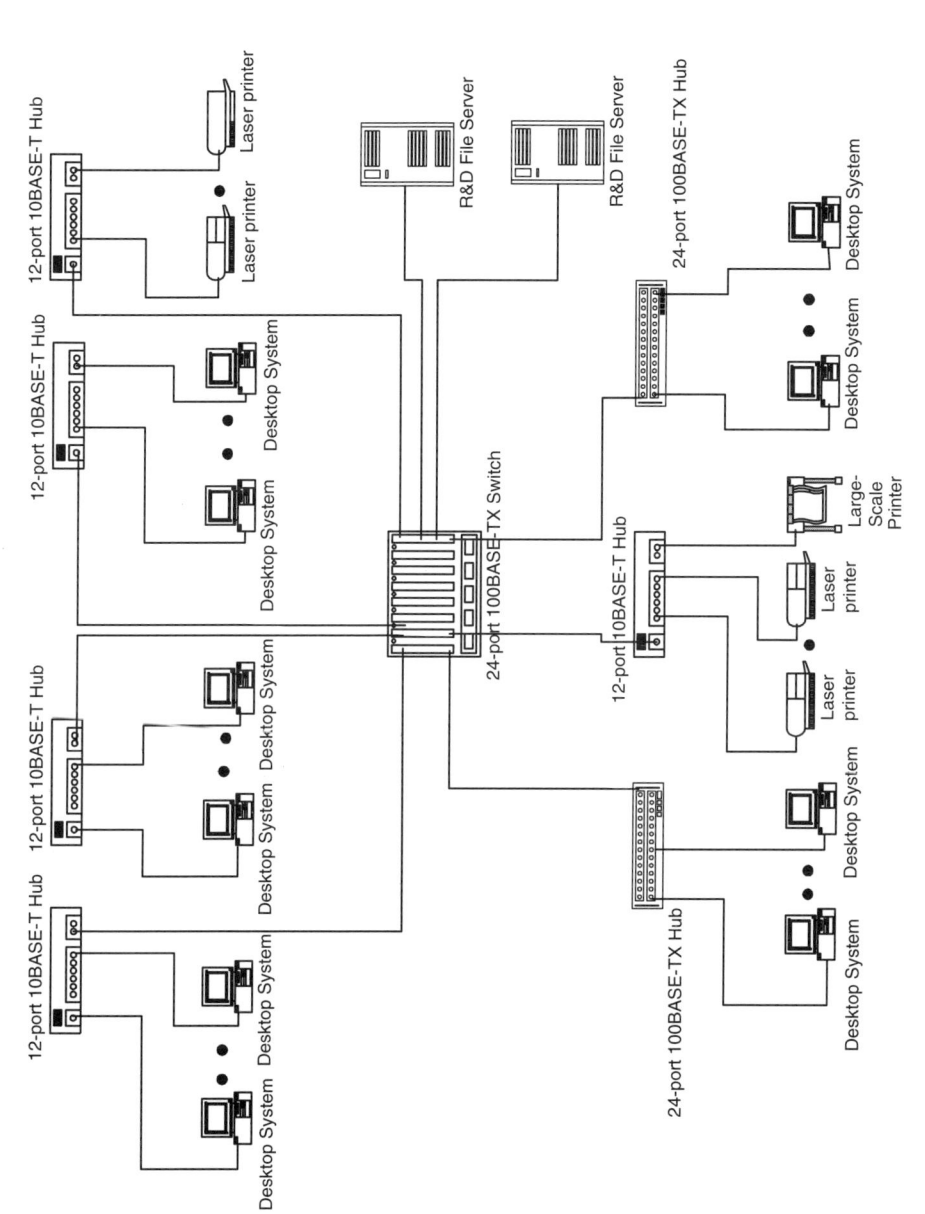

**Figure 10-2:** Proposed network

No major sources of RFI or EMI were found in the ceiling or walls, which verified that CAT5 twisted pair cable would be more than adequate to cable the site. The selection was based on the length of the runs, the longest being only 280 feet, and the lack of electrical disturbances such as EMI and RFI.

The site drawing was updated to note where all of the network plates would be for each office and cubicle and where the "stubs," a piece of conduit in the wall to run the cable down, would be located.

With the site drawing now complete, everything was double-checked against the prints for accuracy.

This case study was selected because of its simplicity. It is designed to help you to see how each step of the design was accomplished. The case study is continued at the end of Chapter 11 to help document installation.

## 10.15 Review Questions

1. What are the three basic rules of design?

2. Writing down every little thing takes a lot of time. Why do it?

3. What would you have done differently in the case study? Why?

# Chapter 11

# Installation

## 11.1 Introduction

With the design complete, you are now faced with the sometimes frightening task of installing the network. While this task can be, and more often than not is, overwhelming, it does not have to be. The very first step is to take a deep breath and remember the old saying, *"The journey of a thousand miles starts with just one step."* With this thought in mind, start at the beginning, work through the process one step at a time, and you will succeed at completing this arduous task.

The installation of a network encompasses many functions and efforts:

- Dealing with the local officials, such as planning offices and inspectors.
- Working with other contractors.
- Planning the work flow.

- Organizing labor.
- Making sure the correct supplies, in the correct quantities, arrive at the correct time.
- Managing changes in scheduling.
- Making sure the cables are run properly and the connectors are installed correctly.
- Documenting the whole process.

The first task of installing a network is deciding whether or not to contract out any of the job.

## 11.2 The Decision to Contract

There are many things to consider when selecting a contractor to assist in the installation of your network. The first thing to consider is if you want to contract just a part of the project or use internal resources to perform the entire task.

The decision whether to use a contractor, in-house personnel, or a combination of both is primarily based on three factors: the scope of the project, the size and qualifications of the available labor pool, and the ability to manage the project.

### 11.2.1 Scope of Project

The scope of each project is driven by three main factors. These are the size of the project, time constraints, and budget restrictions.

## *Size of Project*

The size of a project is based on several factors. These include the number of node connections being established, the phase that the construction is in when you are scheduled to start work, the type of media selected, and the physical space involved.

The number of node connections to be established is simply a count of every location where a node may at some time be attached to the network.

The phase of construction when you are scheduled to start is very important. If the construction is not complete, you will want to start your installation before the walls are closed, but after all of the framing and most of the mechanical are completed. The mechanical aspects of construction include plumbing, electrical, and HVAC.

If the construction is completed, you will have to deal with certain issues, such as how to get cabling into the walls.

The type of medium selected has a bearing in that handling and installation techniques are specific to the medium type. Each handling technique will have a different cost in time. For example, the installation of glass fiber-optic cable will require considerably more time than coax.

The physical space involved with the installation becomes increasingly important as multiple floors or buildings become involved.

## *Time Constraints*

Often the amount of time allotted to complete a network installation is marginal at best. To make the best case for more time, you will need a clear realistic picture of how long each phase of construction will take. Some of the critical questions are

- How long will it take to get the materials?
- How much time will be allotted to each task?
- How long will proper testing take?

With these questions answered, draw up a Gantt chart of the project.

To get this information you may need to hire a networking consultant who understands the installation phase. Take care not to underestimate the time necessary to install a network properly.

**Budget Restrictions**

Rarely is enough money allotted in the budget for the installation of a network. The cost projections and what management expects to spend are most commonly diametrically opposed. The best thing to do is to make sure that management has a realistic picture of the monetary and time requirements necessary to accomplish the job.

## 11.2.2 Size and Qualifications of Labor Pool

The size of your labor pool is something only you can determine, but as you are making the decision, consider the qualifications of your available labor. The installation of a network is not something to be taken lightly. Remember, your network will provide a critical link in the information flow of your department or company.

## 11.2.3 The Final Decision

As you consider all of these factors, be aware that whether the project is kept in-house or contracted out, someone from your organization will have to be the manager. This project management will require time spent on a variety of activities including designing, design review, research of permit and code requirements, materials planning, scheduling of materials, scheduling of labor, verifying that the work is being performed to specification, and problem resolution. These will only be a few of your time expenses. Take care not to fall into the trap of not allowing enough time to manage the project.

If you do not have someone at your disposal who can properly manage all of the aspects of the project, then you are on your way to hiring a professional contractor. If you can manage the project, carefully consider the scope of the project, the size, and qualifications of your available labor pool (see Fig. 11.1).

# 11.3 Selecting a Contractor

When you have made the decision to subcontract some portion of the project out, you have the dubious pleasure of selecting a contractor. Before embarking on this journey, clarify just what you want the contractor to do for you.

- Do you want the contractor to provide all labor and materials?
- Who will be responsible for permits and code restrictions?
- Who will schedule the materials?
- Who is responsible for communicating requirements to the general contractor?

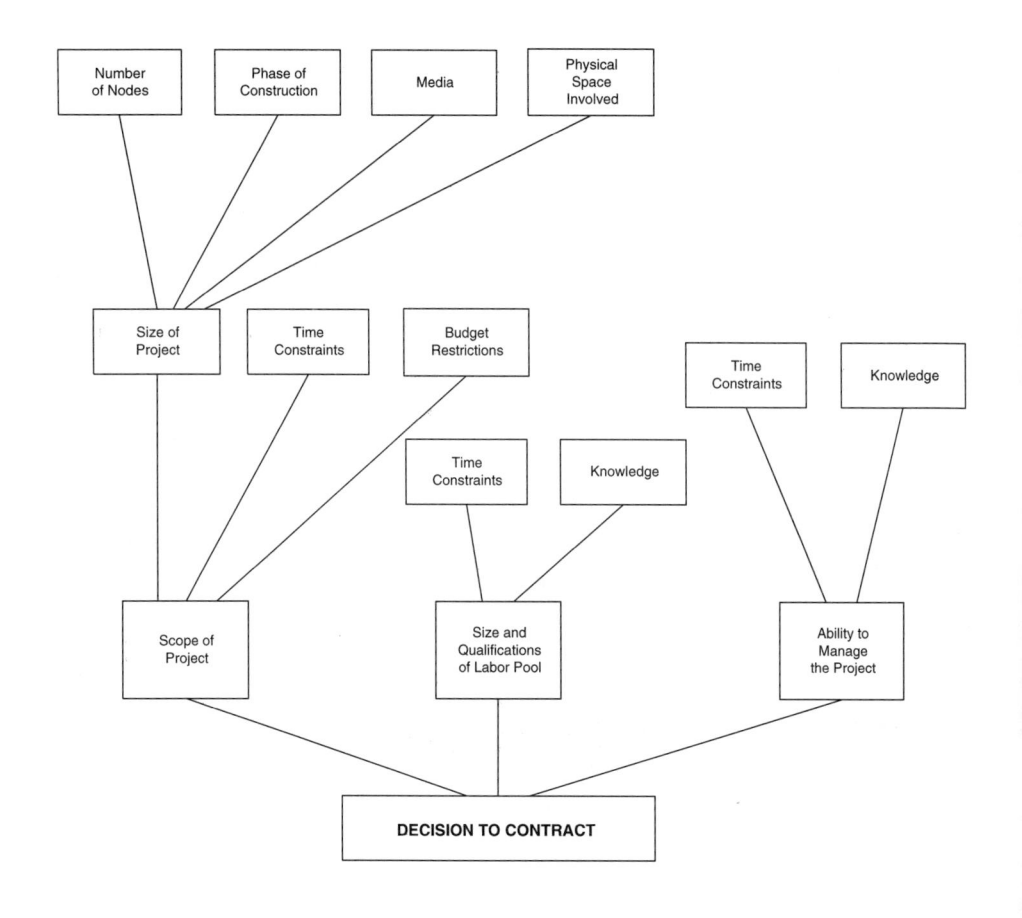

**Figure 11.1:** Decision tree

*11.3 Selecting a Contractor*

Once you have a written a list of exactly what you want the contractor to do for you and what you are planning to handle using your company resources, it is time to start calling contractors.

## 11.3.1 Where to Look for a Contractor

There are two main sources to find contractors. The first and perhaps the most obvious is the phone book. The second source for locating a contractor is the best—use referrals.

To get referrals call companies in your area that have networks, or seem likely candidates for networks, and ask for the person in charge of the network. Another excellent referral source would be local user groups. Also, manufacturers often have a list of contractors that they know of in given geographical areas.

Once you have a list of contractors, start calling them and making appointments to interview them at your office.

## 11.3.2 How to Interview a Contractor

With your marked blueprints and expectations list at hand, meet with each proposed contractor. Explain to the contractor the scope of the job, what parts you are going to handle, and which parts you expect them to handle. Be very specific about the time restrictions and insist on a completion time that will allow for a margin of error. Ask each prospective contractor the following questions:

### ABOUT THEIR COMPANY

- How many years has the company been in business?
- Are they licensed with the state?
- Are they bonded?
- Are they insured? For how much?
- How many employees do they currently employ?
- What are the employees' qualifications?
- Do they have all of the necessary tools to accomplish this job?

### ABOUT THEIR WORK

- Will they provide a reference list?
- How many jobs of relative size have they completed?
- How many jobs have they done with your specified media type(s)?
- Are any of these companies on their reference list?
- If not, will they provide some of them as references?
- Can they accomplish the job ahead of schedule? (This provides a pad.)
- When can they provide you with a written proposal? (Provide a reasonable deadline.)

## 11.3.3 Making the Final Decision

Your final decision on which contractor to select will depend on how each contractor rated in your interview, by their answers to your questions, and by the feel you get as to who will "work with you."

It is important that the contractor be able to prove significant ability to perform their part of the contract with a superior level of quality. It is almost equally as important that you be able to communicate effectively with the prospective contractor.

If you had trouble in the interview with a contractor's attitude note it. If a contractor's attitude hampers their ability to communicate effectively, it is very likely there will be more trouble as the job progresses. The more the contractor will have to deal with a general contractor on the construction site, the more important communication skills and positive attitude become.

It cannot be overstated that the relationship to the general contractor must never be put in jeopardy because of attitudes or poor communication skills.

After making your final selection of a contractor, it is considered a courtesy to notify all of the other bidding contractors that they were not chosen for the project.

## 11.4 The First Step

Meet with the contractor and any personnel from your company who are helping to manage the installation. In this first planning meeting make sure that each member of your newly formed Installation Planning Committee (IPC) has a copy of both the marked and unmarked blueprints. Review each member's area of responsibility and identify where overlap exists. Stress communications with the IPC. Clearly identify the individual(s) who can make final decisions in a crunch situation.

Also in the first meeting, discuss the time table for the project and make sure that each member understands the time restraints. Make sure that everyone understands that clear documentation of all aspects of the job is a requirement, not a suggestion. Identify dependencies and lay out the first steps toward implementation. Lastly, schedule the next meeting.

As the project continues, meet often with those involved. Identify problems and possible solutions.

## 11.5 What to Watch For

One of the most important tasks in the management of an installation is walking the job. While walking the job, keep your eyes open for quality. Do not tolerate activities that detract from the quality of your end product. Watch for careless actions and take your stand against them.

Make sure the documentation is being done consistently. The last thing you want to hear is "yeah, uh we'll get to it later." Make sure notes are legible and drawings are accurate. This documentation is going to save you trouble later.

Make sure your media is being handled with care. Do not let the media be tugged with force that appears excessive. If it needs that much force to pull, then maybe there is another problem. Take the time to correct it now. It will save you magnitudes of time later.

Watch the way connectors are being put on. Insist on perfect connections. Yes, the job of connectorizing the ends of the cables is tremendously tedious, but that is the job at hand. Make sure that no effort is spared to make a perfect connection every time. Remember, bad connections will be one of your worst nightmares—hard to find, intermittent, and terribly devastating to the confidence of your management and users in the stability of a network.

# 11.6 Documentation

Documentation should include notes, drawings, measurements, and splice locations. It is important to remember that the more detailed your notes, the easier your life will be in the future.

I like to use a stitched "lab" style notebook. Each page is numbered and has a graph pattern. Each day, place the date at the top of a fresh page.

## 11.6.1 Notes

Keep notes on phone calls, verbal commitments, questions, answers, problems, and solutions. Always make note of who, what, when, where, and why.

## 11.6.2 Drawings

Keep a notebook with a copy of every drawing of the facility you are cabling. Each change in the layout of the facility usually results in a new drawing. Get a copy and keep it. Date all of the drawings and keep them in chronological order.

Make sure that each cable placed is detailed on your drawings. As special circumstances or obstacles are encountered, make note of them on your drawings.

As the job draws to a close, make a master print that shows all of the cable locations and note all of the special circumstances and obstacles.

### 11.6.3 Measurements

As each cable is pulled, keep as accurate a record as possible of the amount of cable used for the run. Keep these distances marked on your drawings. There are devices available that will keep track of the length of cable used as it is pulled off a reel or out of a box. These counters are probably the best bet for accurate measurements.

## 11.7 Getting Ready

Preparing for the installation of the network is another somewhat tedious task that will reward you with great reduction in troubleshooting headaches and installation "gotchas."

## 11.7.1 Getting Ready Step 1

The first step in preparation is making sure that those doing the installation are clear on their objectives and how to carry out their tasks. Make sure each member of your team knows who to contact in the event of a problem.

## 11.7.2 Getting Ready Step 2

Step 2 is to make sure that those who are going to put on the connectors have plenty of practice and are very competent before they start putting connectors on the actual network. This will cost time and money for the wasted connectors but will result in a more consistent quality of connection.

## 11.7.3 Getting Ready Step 3

Step 3 is to test the cable in the box or on the spool. The best way to test the cable is to use a Time Domain Reflectometer (TDR). The TDR is a specialized piece of equipment that is able to look at a cable and report on total length. If there are shorts or opens, it will detect where in the cable they are. If you lack the availability of a TDR, you can use a Volt Ohm Meter (VOM) or a hand-held cable tester to check the continuity of the cable. Fiber-optic cable will require specialized tools.

CHAPTER 11 | *Installation*

## *Testing with a TDR*

The TDR (Time Domain Reflectometer) is a specialized testing tool. This tool can ask as many questions as it can generate answers. In the hands of an inexperienced user, the information provided is usually fairly useless because of the user's inability to interpret it. In the hands of an experienced user, this testing tool can be one of the most helpful tools available for a wire medium.

The principle of the TDR is much akin to radar. A signal is transmitted down the cable and the reflection of that signal is displayed as a waveform, containing information regarding the cable. The information provided will include the length of the cable, the distance of any shorts or opens from the TDR, the presence of transceivers, the distance to an excessive bend in the cable, barrel connectors, and terminators.

Before purchasing a TDR, you should strongly consider renting one. If you are hiring a contractor for some portion of the job, check with them and see if they have one that could be provided.

## *Testing with a VOM*

The first step is to make sure that the conductors at both ends of the cable are not touching. Then, at one end use the VOM to make sure that a reading of infinity is registered on the highest ohms scale on the meter.

**NOTE:** On some meters the infinity reading in the ohms scale will result in an OL, or overload, indication. This test will show that there are no shorts in the cable.

## 11.7 Getting Ready

The second test is to terminate one end of the coax cable with a connector and attach a 50-ohm terminator, or short the individual wires of each pair of the twisted pair cable together without shorting the pairs. Then, at the other end, you should receive a reading of slightly more than 50 ohms but not more than 60 ohms for the coax cable and slightly more than 0 ohms on the shorted twisted pairs. This test proves that the conductors of the cable have no opens.

### *Testing with a Hand-Held Tester*

This tester couples the usefulness of the VOM and TDR into an easy-to-use package. You will definitely want one of these in your toolbox.

The hand-held cable tester is extremely versatile in that the operator does not have to be concerned with knowing the Vp of most of the common types of cables. Most of the units are a combination of menu and dial driven, helping them to be much more intuitive than other types of test equipment.

The hand-held cable tester will test for shorts, opens, and termination like the VOM. It will also test for length like the TDR. These units will also test for Near End Crosstalk (NEXT), noise, and characteristic impedance of a cable.

Near End Crosstalk (NEXT) occurs when the signals on one pair of cable are being detected on another pair. The main causes of NEXT are split cable pairs, untwisted pairs, or improper cladding. It is because of the problems with NEXT that the use of parallel conductor type cables, like flat satin or ribbon cables, is not permitted.

Noise is any signal on the cable that was not originally transmitted. Noise that is induced from other pairs is considered NEXT. The cables used in the LAN act as antennae for inductive noise from sources like fluorescent lights and electric motors.

Characteristic impedance of a cable is the measurement of resistance that a high-frequency signal experiences as it is transmitted down the cable. The impedance of a cable is not the same as dc resistance, which can be measured with a VOM. The capacitive and inductive characteristics of a cable are the main factors in the cable's characteristic impedance. The conductor size, spacing, and insulating material between the conductors determine the capacitive and inductive properties of a cable.

If the characteristic impedance of a cable changes, a portion of the signal traveling down the cable will be reflected back toward the source. The larger the discontinuity or change in the characteristic impedance, the more the signal is reflected. The concern with new cable is to make sure that there is not significant cable distortion caused by compression. The compression of a coaxial cable causes the spacing of the center conductor and the shield to be reduced, thus changing the capacitive and inductive properties of that section of cable.

## 11.8 Starting the Installation

### 11.8.1 Installation—Step One

The first step of installation is to install all of the cable support hardware. This hardware includes the conduits and cable troughs.

## 11.8.2 Installation—Step Two

Step two is to run all of the cable. This sounds easy and sometimes it is. To avoid problems in later stages, consider some of the following rules:

### *Rule 1*

Identify the cable ends with a number or letter designation before beginning the pull. Most electrical distributors have kits available for numbering cable ends. These kits consist of pads of preprinted numbers, which are cut so they can be wrapped around a cable.

First number the end of the cable that will be pulled and then number the box or roll being pulled from.

### *Rule 2*

When running the cable, work to avoid pulling it or another bundle of cables over a stationary cable, as this will result in friction burn of the stationary cable's insulation.

### *Rule 3*

Avoid the use of force when pulling cable. There will be times when the cable bundles will be heavy and hard to pull, but when the resistance to pulling requires excessive force, there is a problem. When you encounter heavy resistance to a pull, take the time to investigate the cause and spend the time to not stress the cable.

## Rule 4

Always attach your cables out of harm's way. Cables left to dangle where they may be in another contractor's way, are cables that are in harm's way. Take the time to properly trim out the job.

## Rule 5

Leave a little slack. Yes, the cable should be neat and out of harm's way, but leave a foot or two of extra slack at the end of each run. This will provide the opportunity to replace cable ends if there is a problem without making the cable stretch.

### 11.8.3 Installation—Step Three

With the cabling in place, the next step is to install the connectors. This step is extremely critical. A bad or flaky connection will cause you endless grief.

Each connector should be installed as if it were the most critical one on the entire network. Each connector is like a link in a chain. The chain is only as strong as its weakest link. Because of this, each link or connector is the most critical one in the network. This process will prove tedious, but stick to your guns and make sure every connection is perfect.

### 11.8.4 Installation—Step Four

The fourth step of the installation is the testing of each leg or segment. Again, a TDR, VOM, or hand-held tester may be employed as described earlier.

*11.8 Starting the Installation*

**NOTE:** TDRs are not always accurate for short lengths of cables. Consult your user guide for your TDR and use alternate methods of testing for cable lengths that are shorter than the minimum length for accurate measurement by your TDR.

## 11.8.5 Installation—Step Five

Using a tester, make sure the power in each of the equipment closets is wired properly. The first test should be with a VOM to assure that the voltage is at the proper level. The second test is with an electrical wiring tester to make sure that the power is wired correctly. You should consider having an Uninterruptible Power Source (UPS) in your equipment closet for supplying power to your network hardware.

When the power has been verified, install all of the hardware, routers, bridges, and repeaters, and run any self-tests provided for the equipment.

## Getting Started—Installation Step Six

With the hardware installed and tested, you can now start to make all of the connections to the hardware. Make sure that there are no open loops and that all lines requiring termination are properly terminated.

## 11.9 Case Study

For this installation case study, I will again use the small manufacturing firm that I used in the design chapter.

After the network had been designed and the costs approved, we were ready to begin the installation.

### Getting Ready—Step 1

To prepare for the installation, a meeting was called with all of the people involved. The first order of business was to define who was managing what and who to look for if there was a problem or question. With that resolved, a plan for the installation was laid out. Each person was assigned their initial tasks and everyone was sure that they had a clear understanding of what was expected.

### Getting Ready—Step 2

A cabling contractor was hired to install the network. The contractor personnel were very experienced with the tools and techniques required for the installation of the connectors, so no training or practice for the IT personnel was necessary. Therefore, the second step was to pretest all the cable.

To pretest the cable, a hand-held cable tester was used. To pre-test the rolls of cable, both ends of the cable had a RJ45 connectors attached. The connector on one end provided the ability to connect one piece of the test equipment and the other end plugged directly into the hand-held tester. No shorts or opens were found and all cables passed the tests available on the tester.

*11.9 Case Study*

# Installation—Step 1

The next task was to install all of the cable support hardware. The cable troughs were installed. Conduits were also installed inside every wall where there was to be a computer. In every wall where a conduit was installed, a special outlet box was also installed. This box, often called a "tiger grip" box, was plastic and had wings that would extend and grip the drywall to hold the box firmly in place. Lastly, the short stubs of three-inch pipe were stubbed through the firewall and the firewall sealed around the pipes.

## *Conduit Installation*

The installation of the conduit was the most difficult part of the support hardware installation. For each location, a small hole, approximately two-inches square, was cut in the top plate of the wall and another hole, approximately two-inches wide by four-inches high, was cut directly below the first, at the bottom of the wall, twelve inches from the floor.

After the holes were cut, a 10-foot piece of precut, 1-inch inside diameter, flexible plastic conduit was pulled down from the hole in the top plate to the top of the outlet box by the use of a pull string.

To pull the conduit, a large nut was tied to one end of a 15-foot length of nylon cord. With one person on a ladder and one on the floor next to the opening of the box, the person on the ladder dropped the end of the cord with the nut down the hole cut in the top plate. The person on the floor then pulled the end of the cord out of the hole made by the outlet box. The person on the ladder then taped the cord to one end of the flexible conduit and the person on the floor pulled the conduit down with the string. When the conduit end was in place, the tape was removed and the end was fastened to the stud with bailing wire. Then, the person on the ladder tied down the top of the conduit with bailing wire. By tying down both ends of the conduit, they assured that it would not slide into the wall or curl away from the box. Finally, a pull string was installed in each tube with the top end of the string tied off to the bailing wire, to which the tube was originally attached. The bottom of the string was pulled through the back of the box, and the box was installed. These steps were repeated for every opening.

## *Firewall Penetration*

Where the firewall had to be penetrated, two pieces of three-inch inside diameter, metal pipe were cut to two feet and put through the wall. After the lengths of pipe were put in place, a fireproof sealer was used to seal the remaining gaps. These conduits provided a permanent path for cables to be run through the walls, without compromising the integrity of the fire wall.

## Installation—Step 2

With all of the support hardware in place, the next step was the installation of the cable. The loose end of each box was marked with a unique number that was also placed on the same box. Where a box was used more than once, a new number was assigned to the cable and box each time.

Multiple cables were pulled together. Before cutting any of the cables, a minimum of 12 inches of slack were left at the box end and several feet of extra slack were left on the end where the patch panels were to be installed.

## Installation—Step 3

With the cables in place, the next task was terminating all the cable ends. Extra care was taken to assure less than one-half of an inch of wire was untwisted at each end, for the purposes of termination, in order to stay within the category five specifications.

## Installation—Step 4

After the installation of the connectors, the testing of the segments began. A hand-held tester was used. Every cable was numbered and all of the statistics for the cable were recorded. These statistics included length and NEXT measurements.

## Installation—Step 5

In the equipment closet where the hubs and switches were to be installed, the line voltage was tested and found to be acceptable. The next line electrical test was for proper wiring. Using a common plug tester, it was determined that the outlets were wired properly.

With the knowledge that the electrical power was okay, the equipment was rack-mounted and plugged in. All of the segments were connected.

## 11.10 Chapter 11 Review Questions

1. What are the three primary factors that the decision to hire a contractor might be based on?
2. What are the three main factors that determine the scope of a project?
3. What are some of the activities involved in the management of an installation project?
4. Of what four things should your documentation consist?
5. What would you have done differently in the case study? Why?

# Chapter 12

# Maintenance

## 12.1 Introduction

One of the first laws learned in physical science is the law of entropy. Simply stated, it says that anything left to its own devices will eventually end in disorder. This laws applies not only to the physical sciences, but also to the science of computers. A network that is not actively maintained and managed will eventually fall into a state of total disorder.

The importance of maintaining a network is often overlooked by management. Your first task in maintaining your network is to convince your management that the maintenance is important enough to warrant the expense for the appropriate and necessary tools.

Network maintenance is performed at two levels: connectivity and equipment. At each of these levels there are two types of maintenance: preventative and corrective. It is obvious that corrective maintenance is necessary, but quite often preventative maintenance is completely overlooked.

Network management is the proactive monitoring of your network. There are two goals of network management. The first is to be able to predict problems before they arise and thus be able to circumvent them. The second is security. If the network has any connection to a public network, or there is any other reason for concern that someone might attempt to violate the network, proper management techniques will assist in spotting problems.

## 12.2 Connectivity Maintenance

Connectivity maintenance has to do with maintaining media and connections. The energies expended in this effort include tracking down shorts and opens, noise, and troublesome connections. In the last few years new test equipment has been released onto the market. This new test equipment provides greater efficiency in the testing and evaluation of media.

There are three main types of equipment used in the testing and evaluation of a LAN. They are the Volt Ohm Meter (VOM), Time Domain Reflectometer (TDR), and the hand-held cable tester, often referred to as a cable meter, or cable scanner.

### 12.2.1 The VOM

The Volt Ohm Meter (VOM) is used to measure voltages, currents, and resistance in circuits. Most of these meters are now digital. The main use of this meter is the basic function test of the media. The meter will indicate shorts, opens, and resistance (for checking termination). The

*12.2 Connectivity Maintenance*

meter will not aid in determining how long a cable is, if there is noise present, or if some other malady exists on the cable. The VOM makes a good quick check but is not usable for comprehensive testing.

## 12.2.2 The TDR

The Time Domain Reflectometer (TDR) is the original testing tool for media. This tool will work with most copper cables. The TDR works like radar. It transmits a pulse down the cable and measures the time from transmission to reception of the reflection. From this time, the TDR is able to calculate the length of the cable. If the cable is terminated, then the TDR will not function properly.

The TDR is typically the most difficult type of equipment to use. It requires the operator to have more knowledge than for the other types of test equipment. One of the pieces of information that the operator must know is the Velocity of Propagation (Vp), also referred to as the Nominal Velocity of Propagation (NVP). Vp is measured as a percentage of the speed of light. Each cable type has its own Vp. For example, RG58 A/U has a Vp of 0.66.

Another skill the TDR operator must possess is the ability to interpret the results of the tests performed. The TDR displays waveforms indicative of the signal traveling down the cable. Each signal shape has special meaning.

## 12.2.3 The Hand-Held Cable Tester

Equipment manufacturers realized the needs of the people in the field who were trying to use the test equipment. These people needed something that was fast, intuitive, and multifaceted. The response was the hand-held cable tester. This tester couples the usefulness of

CHAPTER 12                                                                Maintenance

the VOM and TDR into an easy-to-use package. You will definitely need one of these in your toolbox.

The hand-held cable tester is extremely versatile in that the operator does not have to be concerned with knowing the Vp of most of the common types of cables. Most of the units are a combination of menu- and dial-driven, helping them to be much more intuitive than other types of testing equipment.

The hand-held cable tester will test for shorts, opens, and termination, like the VOM. It will also test for length like the TDR. These units will also test for Near End Crosstalk (NEXT), noise, and characteristic impedance of a cable.

Near End Crosstalk (NEXT) is when the signals on one pair of cable are being detected on another pair. The main causes of NEXT are split cable pairs, untwisted pairs, or improper cladding. It is because of the problems with NEXT that the use of parallel conductor type cables, like flat satin or ribbon cables, is discouraged.

Noise is any signal on the cable that was not originally transmitted. Noise that is induced from other pairs is considered NEXT. The cables used in the LAN are like antennas for inductive noise from sources like fluorescent lights and electric motors.

Characteristic impedance of a cable is the measurement of resistance that a high-frequency signal experiences as it is transmitted down the cable. The impedance of a cable is not the same as dc resistance, which can be measured with a VOM. The capacitive and inductive characteristics of a cable are the main factors in the characteristic impedance of a cable. The conductor size and spacing, and the insulating material between the conductors, determine the capacitive and inductive properties of a cable.

If the characteristic impedance of a cable changes, a portion of the signal traveling down the cable will be reflected back toward the source. The larger the discontinuity, or change in the characteristic impedance, the more of the signal that is reflected. The most common causes of discontinuity are mismatched cable types. For example, a section of RG62 is placed in-line with some RG58 mismatched termination, placing a 93-ohm terminator on a section of RG58, and cable distortion caused by compression. The compression of a coaxial cable causes the spacing of the center conductor and the shield to be reduced, thus changing the capacitive and inductive properties of that section of cable.

## 12.2.4 Connectivity Preventative Maintenance

When any new segment of cable is to be introduced into a LAN, that cable section should be thoroughly tested prior to its installation.

First, the cable segment should be tested for shorts and opens, characteristic impedance, and NEXT before the cable is installed. After the cable is installed and before the equipment is connected, these tests should be repeated. The cable length should be measured and the cable marked. Finally there should be a master drawing that documents the physical locations of the cable, another that reflects the logical connection, and an entry made in a log book of the characteristics of the cable, at least the length and NEXT.

Every effort should be made to ensure that the cable is not under any tension. Also, the cable should be placed in such a way that accidental severance, crushing, or other mishap is minimized. Finally, the cable should be installed so that induced noise from fluorescent lighting and electrical motors is not a problem.

Routing cables in cable troughs or through D-rings, well away from other mechanical facility equipment, such as air ducts, electrical, and plumbing fixtures will reduce the likelihood of a facility's maintenance creating problems.

### 12.2.5 Connectivity Corrective Maintenance

When a connectivity problem occurs, disconnect all of the attached equipment and test the cable for shorts, opens, characteristic impedance, NEXT, and cable length. A good hand-held cable tester will indicate the distance to a short or open.

The typical causes of connectivity problems include common mishaps like someone tripping over a cable, damage by hungry rodents, non-requested "helpful" assistance of other office workers lengthening cables to workstations, and damage caused during a facility's maintenance.

## 12.3 Equipment Maintenance

Equipment maintenance is the care of the equipment that is part of the LAN. This equipment includes transceivers, repeaters, bridges, routers, gateways, and network interface cards (NICs).

### 12.3.1 Equipment Preventative Maintenance

Preventative maintenance for equipment is mainly accomplished at installation. Equipment should be installed according to the manufacturers' specifications in order to prevent problems that they have foreseen. Also, it is imperative to make sure that equipment fans are not only not blocked but also have adequate access to cool air. Heat is one of equipment's biggest enemies. Another cause of equipment-related problems comes from power problems. Make sure equipment is plugged into a clean power source. Sharing power lines with copiers, laser printers, arc welders, refrigerators, and so forth, may cause significant power-related problems with equipment. These power problems may result is erroneous operation of the equipment or complete failure of the equipment.

Checking equipment on a semiregular basis for heat and cleanliness will also help to prevent troubles. Equipment acts like a dirt magnet. The dirt will clog up air vents and cover components. This will cause heating problems that can lead to equipment failure.

### 12.3.2 Equipment Corrective Maintenance

When equipment fails, the usual method of repair is replacement of the card-level components within the equipment that failed. Difficulty often lies in tracking down what has failed. Network management tools often lend a helpful hand in the isolation of equipment failure. Also, many manufacturers have status indicators on the equipment.

## 12.4 Network Management

The network should be monitored daily. Monitoring can be done in two ways: with special equipment and/or software or manually. The daily monitoring of a network will help to establish a history of network performance. As the administrator becomes familiar with the normal operation of the network, they will be able to spot changes in network performance. Changes may include a dramatic increase in network traffic, an increase in the error rate, or unexpected traffic patterns in off hours. These changes alert the administrator to possible problems. The problems may be security related, early signs of controller or transceiver failure, or an early sign of network overloading.

By detecting problems early, the administrator can manage the situation in a proactive fashion, possibly avoiding any serious downtime or continuance of security breach.

The initial investment of time and training to become proficient with tools often results in defaulting to the use of a manual method. Management needs to understand that the LAN will soon become a major part of how the company processes data. Major assets will eventually be connected to the network. These assets may be intellectual data, competitive data, financial data, or systems whose functions are shared by network users. The ability to routinely process data as well as assets are at risk when network management is not taken seriously.

### 12.4.1 Using Special Equipment and/or Software

The two major automated ways of knowing the health of your network are the use of a protocol analyzer and the use of special network monitoring software.

A protocol analyzer is a computer system that is attached to the network. The analyzer operates in what is called promiscuous mode. That is, it looks at all of the packets on the network, not just the ones directed at it. The protocol analyzer gathers information from the packets. The information gathered includes source, destination, type of protocol used, and errors.

## 12.4 Network Management

Network analysis software provides a different level of usable information based on the package used. For example, one manufacturer has an analysis package that is sold with their hardware. This package provides information about the loading of the network and error information. Some packages cannot provide information on a per node basis unless one of the manufacturer's Ethernet cards is installed in each node. Tools that use SNMP will be able to gather the information on a node by node basis.

Manufacturer-independent analysis software packages are now prevalent on the market. Most of these software packages use a protocol called SNMP (Simple Network Management Protocol) to gather the information about the network. As some equipment does not use SNMP, you must be aware of your network internals before purchasing the package.

Many of the network analysis software packages require the use of special pods, which reside on each subnet of the network. These pods gather information about equipment and traffic on the subnet and transfer that information to the network management node.

Network analysis software packages offer the features of the network analyzer plus the additional feature of being able to store historical data. This data can then be presented in a variety of ways to show many of the functional aspects of your network.

Of the two methods—using a hardware-only tool that can show what is currently happening or using a combination of hardware and software monitoring tools—the use of the hardware and software monitoring tools is superior. There are a few reasons for this superiority. First, the software analysis package collects historical data and most will permit the creation of customized reports from this data.

This software will also permit constant viewing of the network. Icons can be displayed representing different components of the network and when preset limits for traffic or errors are exceeded, the icons will change colors or an audible alarm will be sounded. Finally, the software will permit an online view of the logical connectivity of the network and will encourage the process of keeping the information up-to-date.

While network analysis tools are expensive, they are well worth the cost. The ability to proactively monitor and understand the operational characteristics of your networks will directly result in the ability to avoid and recover from network problems. The information provided will also aid in the planning of network growth and changes.

## 12.4.2 The Manual Method

This method is not very effective, although it is very simple. During the day at regular intervals, the administrator queries several of the users on the network, asking questions about response time, network error messages received, and other difficulties. The major problems with this method are that the users usually become annoyed by the administrator and the quality of information provided can be very inconsistent. For example, network performance will be viewed differently by the same person if the person is having a rough day or if they are having a nice relaxed day.

The goal of this method is the same as the goal of using automated tools—that is, to spot significant changes in network performance that may indicate problems.

*12.5 Case Study*

While this method is not recommended, it should be employed if you can not get the budget for automated tools. It is better to use a system that has some inefficiencies than to do nothing and lose control of the network.

### 12.4.3 Getting Started with Corrective Maintenance

Why do network components fail? While many times there is no obvious answer, possible answers include infant mortality, excessive heat, power fluctuations, thermal fractures of gates, static, or just plain old every day wear and tear. However, no matter the reason for the failure; once one has occurred, it must be corrected.

When there is a failure or indication of a problem on the network, the first thing to do is gather as much information about the failure as possible.

## 12.5 Case Study

This case study is designed to portray only a single problem. However, the concepts used can be applied to almost any problem. If network monitoring tools are being used, then they will most likely provide a very fast view of where the failure is. This case study assumes no monitoring tools.

Tim calls with a complaint that he is unable to transfer a file to the R&D file server.

The first step is to gather as much information about the problem as possible. To get the information about the failure, you will need to get a copy of both the physical and logical network drawings and ask questions.

The network drawings will provide information about the physical connectivity of both Tim and the R&D file server to the LAN. You will be able to ascertain the type of network media each is connected to, what hardware is involved, and how they are connected to each other.

The network drawings show that Tim is connected to the LAN via a 100BASE-TX segment attached to port 4 of a 100BASE-TX hub marked HUB-100-01. The drawings also indicate that the server is connected to the LAN via a connection to the 100BASE-TX switch through a connection to port (see Fig. 12.1).

The next step is to isolate the problem to either the network or system. First, check the hub and the switch to determine if they are functional and if there are any indications of port or line failures. If the hub or switch are experiencing problems, resolve them. If the line appears to be a problem, disconnect from the system and the hub or switch and troubleshoot the cables. If the networking hardware does not provide information about port status, follow the rest of the details below.

If the line or network hardware do not appear to be the problem, the next step is to gather more information about the problem by asking questions.

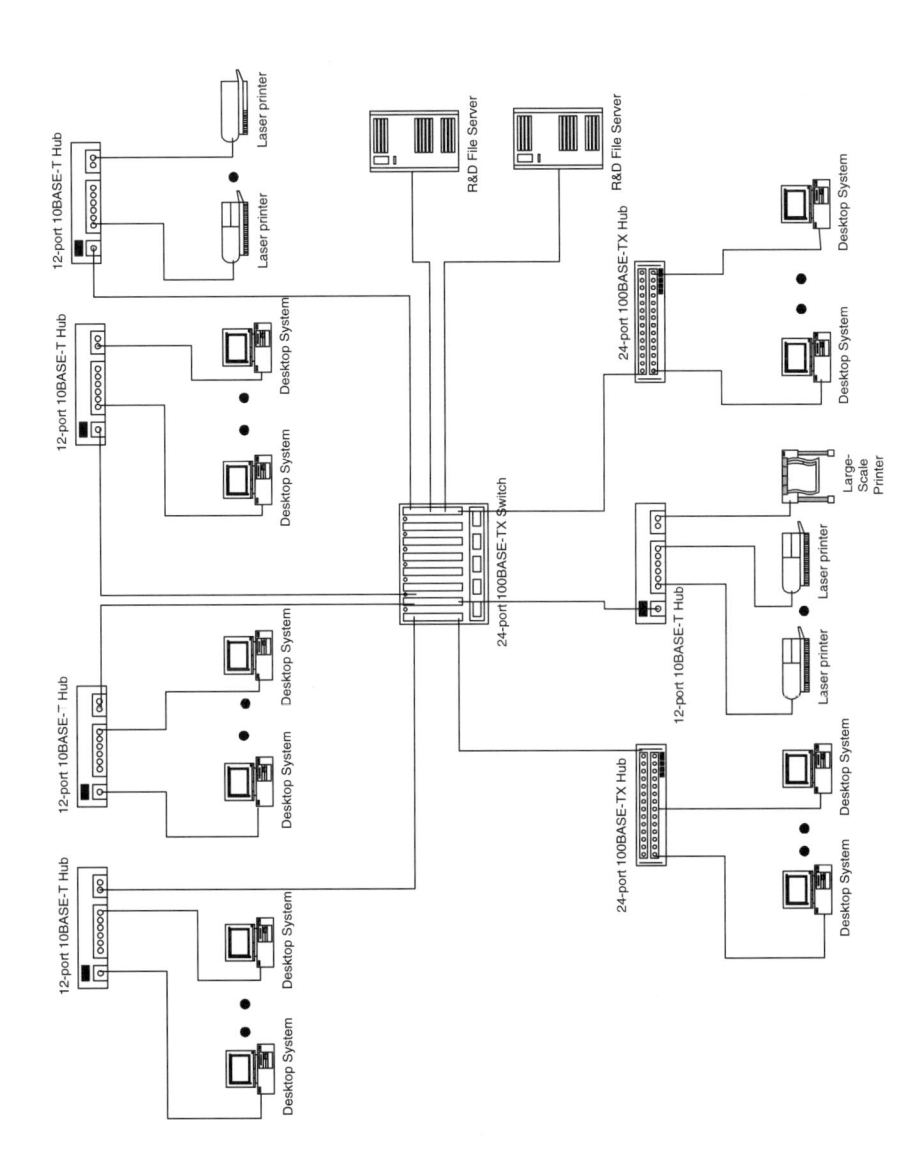

**Figure 12.1:** Logical network connectivity drawing

CHAPTER 12 | Maintenance

Our first question should be, "Was the desired connectivity ever possible and, if so, when was the last time it functioned properly?" If the connectivity never functioned properly, you might involve a systems administrator to determine if Tim has permission to make the connection. The system administrator can also assist with other issues, such as configuration. If the connectivity was previously available and has ceased to function, then you want to know the time of the last successful connection. With the identification of the last time everything appeared to be functioning properly, you can determine if there were any events that have taken place since then that may have caused a problem. Such events would include the relocation of a node, the removal of a node from the network, a node failure, power surges or outages, or accidents with the physical layer (for example someone tripped over a cable in a lab).

The method of determining connectivity relies on the networking protocol being used. When the TCP/IP protocol suite is being used, the most common test for connectivity is the PING protocol. PING sends a packet to the target node with a request for reply.

If Tim is unable to make local access to his own system or another system connected to the same repeater as his system, the problems can include repeater or transceiver problems, a network interface card that has failed, or improper setup of files for the network. It may also be an indication that the network is overloaded and that the call is timing out. The same may be true for the file server.

In our case study, the hub to which Tim's system is connected shows that the connection has failed, indicating a line failure. The cable is disconnected from Tim's system and the hub and thoroughly tested. The test shows the cable to be in the same condition as when installed. All of the connections are put back.

Tim's system is unable to PING to any of the other systems connected to the same repeater as his.

Further study shows that Tim's system had connectivity to the server last night, but connectivity has been unattainable since his arrival this morning. A review of the previous night's schedule shows that some air duct maintenance was performed after Tim left the day before.

Knowing that we tested the cables and that they were functional brings us to checking the system that may have been moved for air duct maintenance. A careful survey of Tim's system shows that the NIC connector has been slightly damaged. Replacement of the NIC resolves this problem.

Granted, this is a simple example, but the concepts of troubleshooting a network are just like the concepts of resolving most problems. The first step is to gather all the information possible about the problem. Then, start to narrow it down. Lastly, divide and conquer.

By taking the time to understand your specific network topology, cabling, hardware, and system software, you will be in the best possible position to isolate and resolve your network problems quickly.

## 12.6 Chapter Summary

The best way to keep a network running smoothly is to take a three-stage approach. First, test all of the components going into your network. Second, install cabling and equipment with a keen awareness for potential spoilers, such as noise-inducing fluorescent light and electric motors. Finally, an active network management strategy that keeps a close watch on the network will warn of potential problems and may give you a head start on problem isolation.

## 12.7 Chapter 12 Review Questions

1. What are the two levels of network maintenance?
2. What are the two types of network maintenance?
3. Name three types of test equipment for troubleshooting network connectivity problems.
4. What is the best way to prevent connectivity corrective maintenance problems?
5. In our case study, what would you have done if our research showed that Tim's system was unable to connect to any other system on the hub to which he is connected?

# Chapter 13

# The Future of Ethernet

## 13.1 Introduction

Software and hardware technologies have been locked in a tremendous battle as they have traded turns bumping into the limitations of the other in their extremely dynamic growth. The results of this process have been an incredible evolution of both hardware and software complexity and functionality.

Early networking was concerned with the rudimentary moving of data between systems. Evolution has brought depth to data. No longer are the data transfers just text and numerical; now we are moving graphics, video, audio, media data, emergency services data, backups, video conferencing, interactive whiteboards, and other types of data, which are rich in various media types. An example of this evolution is that a few years ago scientific and engineering data transfers were mostly text and numbers. Now, this same section of the

CHAPTER 13                                            The Future of Ethernet

market transfers complex CAD drawing files and 3D visualizations of machines, planets, or molecules.

The data being transferred has become and continues to become, more and more complex. Data now in demand to be transmitted onto networks requires that we evaluate its impact on our networking environment. Questions of data type and size, network traffic implications, and networking requirements must be clearly understood.

### 13.1.1 Data Types and Sizes

Data files consisting of a few bytes to terabytes will be the norm for transfer across networks. The standard delivery of large data files is driven by many different markets. As previously discussed, science and engineering are requiring more and more complex and larger data files. There is more and more documentation of every conceivable type now available on networks and it is becoming more prevalent for information to be made available electronically.

Much of the data now being transmitted on the LAN is being made available through the familiar Web browsers that have been mostly associated with the Internet. Companies are setting up Web servers to make information available to employees through this intuitive and familiar interface. The information being made available is in text, video, and audio forms.

The LAN has brought the dispersion of systems and information across workspaces. Backing up data on these systems is often done over the LAN. With growing data file sizes, the demand for backup capacity has skyrocketed. The data files being backed up across the LAN often range from gigabytes to terabytes.

## 13.1 Introduction

Technology like email is now commonplace. Messages from dozens of bytes to gigabytes traverse LANs constantly during the workday. These messages have grown from informational messages to data file attachments and continue to become more complex, permitting the inclusion of audio and video information.

The latest technology to tax networking resources is desktop video conferencing and interactive whiteboarding. These and other video applications require constant data streaming of 1 to 4Mbps. While current LAN technologies will easily handle this for one or two users, when other network traffic is added, it becomes obvious that this is a dramatic demand on networking resources.

### 13.1.2 Network Traffic Implications

The previous section shows that some applications like scientific, engineering, and publications represent potentially large data files that will demand large slices of network bandwidth. Backup of data across networks will also represent large sets of data files moving across the network. Backups, however, will require more bandwidth due to the requirement of moving the data in a restricted amount of time.

Constant data stream applications, such as video conferencing, will require a large volume of data to traverse the network with a level of guaranteed bandwidth availability.

### 13.1.3 Networking Requirements

Differing types of demand on the LAN result in the clear requirement for more bandwidth and higher reliability. The systems that attach to the network will continue to increase in complexity and their ability to deal with more complex data. Applications will also continue to evolve as they become more concerned about interaction with networks.

## 13.2 Strategy for Survival

The increasing demands placed on LANs drive network administrators and managers to evaluate networking technologies that can provide the required bandwidth. While each individual will have different issues, there are some criteria common to most in the decision-making process of selecting a high-speed LAN. These common criteria will best meet the overall business requirements for their organization and have to do with more than just the speed of the network. Other considerations include

- Migration
- Scalability
- Cost of Ownership
- Flexibility

### 13.2.1 Migration

Moving from an existing to a new networking infrastructure without disrupting business is a common goal for not only the network administrator, but senior company management as well.

A series of nondisruptive steps, each of which provides greater capabilities, is the ideal solution. The ability to replace small segments of the infrastructure at a time, with minimal disruption, requires that new pieces maintain compatibility with the old. Sites using Ethernet will be able to migrate from the 10Mbps or 100Mbps networks to a 1Gbps Ethernet. Operation of a mixed environment will not be a significant effort for sites which determine that the increased capabilities are not required sitewide.

## 13.2.2 Scalability

Currently available in both 10Mbps and 100Mbps solutions, Ethernet will add a third tier of performance. Frame format and size will remain unchanged, providing the transparency required to avoid having to make other major networking modifications.

## 13.2.3 Cost of Ownership

Cost of ownership takes into consideration three major components: existing investment, cost for initial purchase, and ongoing support costs.

Migration and scalability play into the concept of protecting the investment in existing technologies. While some of the network may require increased bandwidth, there may be some that do not. The ability to continue using existing infrastructure protects that investment.

While the initial purchase costs are important, the ongoing support costs can eclipse them. If support staff is required to undergo extensive retraining in order to learn about a new networking technology, then those costs need to be considered. There are also intangible costs, such as the loss of the familiarity of the support staff with a particular technology. Another consideration is the test equipment investment. Gigabit Ethernet protects existing investments in infrastructure, training, and tools.

### 13.2.4 Flexibility

The ability to handle varying data types, such as video, is ever increasing in importance as they become used on a regular basis. This flexibility exists today and will only improve with Gigabit Ethernet. A combination of factors contribute to the ability to deal with video:

- Adequate and increasing bandwidth.
- Protocols, such as RSVP, which provide the ability for bandwidth reservation.
- Provision of explicit priority information for packets by new standards.
- The prevalent use of video compression tools, such as MPEG-2.

## 13.3 Gigabit Ethernet Technology Overview

Leveraging the success of 10Mpbs and 100Mpbs Ethernet, Gigabit Ethernet will offer data bandwidth of 1000Mbps, while remaining compatible with the tremendous base of installed Ethernet nodes.

Gigabit Ethernet will initially operate over fiber-optic technologies and twin axial cable, but it is expected to also be able to operate using CAT5 UTP. This technology will continue to use the CSMA/CD MAC methodology or full duplex operation.

The ability to use existing infrastructure and technologies will provide two major benefits:

- Reduction of time to market
- Reduction of cost of ownership

Optical fiber implementation will use existing, readily available components, such as encoding and decoding ICs, optical components, standard single-mode fiber, and 62.5-micron multimode fiber. Using 780-nanometer (nm) short wave-length optical components for implementations over 62.5-micron multimode fiber transmission distances are expected to be from 200 to 550 meters. Using 1300nm (long wavelength) optics on single-mode fiber-supported distances are expected to be 3000 meters.

Use of UTP is based on anticipation of digital signal processing specifications.

## 13.4 Gigabit Migration

The IEEE 802.3z standards committee anticipates five most likely upgrade scenarios:

1. Upgrading switch-to-server connections
2. Upgrading switch-to-switch connections
3. Upgrading a switched Fast Ethernet backbone
4. Upgrading a shared FDDI backbone
5. Upgrading high-performance desktops

Upgrading the connectivity from a switch to application and file servers will provide for increased throughput to, and from, these heavily used resources. This increased throughput will result in a smoothing of network operations for the clients, which may stay on a slower link, 10Mpb or 100Mpbs.

Upgrading the connectivity between switches to 1000Mbps will provide the ability to support greater numbers of 10Mpbs and 100Mbps segments.

Replacing the FFDI concentrator or Ethernet to an FDDI router with a Gigabit Ethernet switch will provide greater capacity throughput for the building or campus.

## 13.5 Conclusion

Gigabit Ethernet is well into the standards process. There has been a substantial amount of effort already put into the initial discussion of standardizing a 1000Mbps Ethernet. In November of 1995, the 802.3 Working Group commissioned the Higher Speed Study Group to consider scaling Fast Ethernet to a higher speed. June 20, 1996, brought approval from the IEEE Standards Board for the Gigabit Ethernet Project Authorization (PAR). The Working Group created the 802.3z Gigabit Ethernet Task Force on July 8, 1996, at the University of Twente in Enschede, Netherlands.

The groundwork has been laid and the IEEE 802.3z Gigabit Ethernet standard will become the foundation for equipment manufacturers and for the implementation of the Gigabit Ethernet equipment and tools.

## 13.6 Chapter Summary

As organizations continue to become dependent on their LANs for day-to-day operations, the selection of networking technology becomes a critical business decision.

### 13.6.1 Major Concepts

Increasing demand on LANs drives network administrators and managers to evaluate networking technologies that meet a broad range of business requirements. There are many considerations to be reviewed during this critical business decision-making process. Issues include

- Migration
- Scalability
- Cost of Ownership
- Flexibility

Moving from an existing to a new networking infrastructure without disrupting business and avoiding having to make other major networking modifications are the major factors when considering migration and scalability.

Cost of ownership is found in all of these considerations. It consists of three major components: existing investment, cost for initial purchase, and ongoing support costs. Migration and scalability play into the concept of protecting the investment in existing technologies. While some of the network may require the increased bandwidth, there may be some that do not. The ability to continue to use existing infrastructure protects that investment.

Initial purchase costs are important. However, the ongoing support costs can eclipse them. Give consideration to the costs and impact of retraining support staff. Do not forget to consider the intangible costs such as loss of the familiarity of the support staff with a particular technology. Take into account the test equipment investment. Gigabit Ethernet protects existing investments in infrastructure, training, and tools.

The flexibility exists today to handle varying data types, such as video, and will only improve with the Gigabit Ethernet.

# Appendix A

# Collision Domain Basics

In the discussion of Ethernet, it is necessary to understand the concept of collision domains. Simply put, this is the domain in which a collision is propagated. All of the equipment in a single collision domain is able to detect that a collision has occurred and, as a result, reschedule their transmission. This prevents any node or nodes from transmitting when there has been a collision. If a node were to keep transmitting when a collision has occurred, the transmission would become corrupted.

Signals are electronic impulses that are carried from the networking equipment (workstations, transceivers, bridges, routers, and so forth) across the physical medium (the cabling) to other networking equipment. While these signals can travel at close to the speed of light, there are inherent delays that occur from the time the signal is transmitted to the time it is finally received by all of the available equipment.

APPENDIX A                                   Collision Domain Basics

The delay that the signal is subjected to is called latency. The delays are incurred as the signal passes through cables and networking equipment and have a significant impact on the collision detection functionality of Ethernet and Fast Ethernet. The impact on the collision detection functionality of Ethernet and Fast Ethernet is the major factor in the determination of Ethernet and Fast Ethernet network diameter rules.

The issue for the network is that the maximum round-trip time cannot exceed 512 bit times (except for gigabit). A bit time is the time that is required to transmit 1 bit of data.

For 10Mbps Ethernet: one bit-time= 1 bit/10Mhz = 100ns.

For Fast Ethernet: one bit-time= 1 bit/100Mhz = 10ns.

# Appendix B

# EIA/TIA Cable Categories

In the discussion of cabling it is important to think in terms of a cabling system. That is, the cable is one of the components that form the entire cabling system. Other components include connectors, outlets, and patch panels. As a cabling system is constructed to meet the specifications of a particular category, it is vital that all of the components meet the same specifications.

There are currently three recognized Unshielded Twisted Pair (UTP) cable categories—CAT3, CAT4, and CAT5.

## B.1 Common Specifications

There are several common characteristics of these three categories of cable. The specific differences are detailed in the sections labeled Category 3, Category 4, and Category 5.

## B.1.1 General

The cable construction is four individually twisted pairs of 24 AWG (American Wire Gauge) enclosed in a thermoplastic jacket. The impedance of the cable is specified to be 100 ohms.

The insulated conductor must be 0.048 inches or 1.22mm maximum in diameter. The overall diameter of the cable is not to exceed 0.25 inches or 6.35mm.

Termination for the cabling is specified as an eight-position modular jack.

When making the connection, the requirement is to minimize the untwisting of the wire pairs and the separation of the individual conductors within each pair.

The maximum pulling tension is specified as 25 lbf (foot pounds).

Cable of greater quality may be used. For example, 22AWG cable that meets these specifications is acceptable.

# B.2 Category 3

A cabling system whose components-specified transmission characteristics are up to 16MHz.

## B.3 Category 4

A cabling system whose components-specified transmission characteristics are up to 20MHz.

Maximum untwisting of cable pairs for the purpose of connecting the connector is specified to be no greater than one inch or 25mm.

## B.4 Category 5

A cabling system whose components-specified transmission characteristics are up to 100MHz.

Maximum untwisting of cable pairs for the purpose of connecting the connector is specified to be no greater than $1/2$ inch or 13mm.

# Appendix C

# Twisted Pair Wiring Diagrams

The standard connector for terminating twisted pair cabling is commonly referred to as an RJ-45 connector (see Fig. C.1).

There are two common standards for making the termination: the EIA/TIA 568A and the EIA/TIA 568B. The IEEE 10BASE-T specification uses EIA specficiations. Both the EIA/TIA 568A and the EIA/TIA 568B standards accomplish the same goal but achieve it slightly differently. The IEEE 10BASE-T and 100BASE-TX, T2, and T4 wiring specifications are specific to the IEEE 10BASE-T and 100BASE-TX, T2, and T4 standards but can be accomplished using either the EIA/TIA 568A or EIA/TIA 568B.

The EIA/TIA 568A and EIA/TIA 568B standards are recommended because they clearly identify the placement of all the conductors. The IEEE 10BASE-T and 100BASE-TX specify a minimum of CAT3-rated cable, which is described in Appendix A. While the specifications require four twisted pairs, only two are used.

*APPENDIX C* *Twisted Pair Wiring Diagrams*

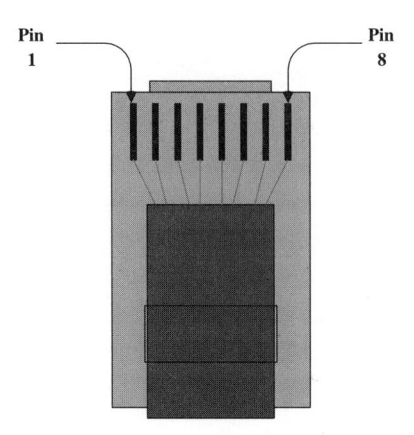

**Figure C.1:** RJ-45 connector

## C.1 10BASE-T, 100BASE-TX, and 100BASE-T2 Pin Assignments

1—TD+
2—TD-
3—RD+
4—Not Used
5—Not Used
6—RD-
7—Not Used
8—Not Used

## C.2  10BASE-T, 100BASE-TX, and 100BASE-T2 Crossover

1—3
2—6
3—1
6—2

## C.3  100BASE-T4 Pin Assignments

1—TX_D1+
2—TX_D1-
3—RX_D2+
4—BI_D3+
5—BI_D3-
6—RX_D2-
7—BI_D4+
8—BI_D4-

*APPENDIX C* *Twisted Pair Wiring Diagrams*

## C.4 100BASE-T4 Crossover

1—3
2—6
3—1
6—2
4—7
5—8
7—4
8—5

# Appendix D

# Abbreviations and Acronyms

The following abbreviations and acronyms may have nothing to do with the Ethernet directly, but they do have to do with the networking and computing industry and thus may prove interesting. Please also note that there may be multiple meanings to any given acronym.

## A

| | |
|---|---|
| ACK | Acknowledgment |
| ACS | Asynchronous Communications Server |
| AFP | AppleTalk Filing Protocol |
| AGS | Asynchronous Gateway Server |
| AMT | Address Mapping Table |
| ANSI | American National Standards Institute |
| API | Applications Program Interface |
| APPC | Applications Program-to-Program Communications |

| APPENDIX D | Abbreviations and Acronyms |
|---|---|

| ARCnet | Attached Resource Computer network |
| ARP | Address Resolution Protocol |
| ARPA | Advanced Research Projects Agency |
| ARPANET | Advanced Research Projects Agency NETwork |
| ARQ | Automatic Repeat Request |
| ASCII | American Standard Code for Information Interchange |
| ATM | Asynchronous Transfer Mode |

# B

| BBN | Bolt Beranek and Newman |
| BIOS | Basic Input/Output System |
| BISYNC | Binary Synchronous Communication |
| BITNET | Because It's Time Network |
| BNC | Bayonet-Neill-Concelman |
| bps | Bits per Second |
| BSC | Binary Synchronous Communication |
| BSD | Berkeley Science Division |

# C

| CCITT | Consultative Committee on International Telephony and Telegraph (no longer exists) |
| CDDI | Copper Distributed Data Interchange |
| CISC | Complex Instruction Set Computing |

| | |
|---|---|
| CLNS | Connectionless-mode Network Service |
| CMIP | Common Management Information Protocol |
| CONS | Connection-mode Network Service |
| CRC | Cyclic Redundancy Check |
| CSMA | Carrier Sense Multiple Access |
| CSMA/CD | Carrier Sense Multiple Access with Collision Detection |
| CSNET | Computer Science Network |
| CSU | Channel Service Unit |

# D

| | |
|---|---|
| DARPA | Defense Advanced Research Projects Agency |
| DCA | Defense Communications Agency |
| DCE | Data Communications Equipment |
| DCE | Distributed Computing Environment |
| DDCMP | Digital Data Communications Message Protocol |
| DDN | Defense Data Network |
| DDP | Datagram Delivery Protocol |
| DIP | Dual In-Line Package |
| DISA | Defense Information Systems Agency |
| DIX | Digital, Intel, Xerox |
| DLC | Data Link Control |
| DMA | Direct Memory Access |
| DOD | Department Of Defense |

| | |
|---|---|
| DOS | Disk Operating System |
| DSAB | Distributed Systems Architecture Board |
| DSAP | Destination Service Access Point |
| DSU | Digital Service Unit |
| DTE | Data Terminal Equipment |
| DTR | Data Terminal Ready |

# E

| | |
|---|---|
| EACK | Extended Acknowledgment |
| EARN | European Academic Research Network |
| EBCIDIC | Extended Binary Coded Decimal Interchange Code |
| ECSA | Exchange Carriers Standards Association |
| EDI | Electronic Data Interchange |
| EGA | Enhanced Graphics Array |
| EGP | Exterior Gateway Protocol |
| EIA | Electronic Industries Associations |
| EISA | Extended Industry-Standard Architecture |
| EOF | End Of File |
| EOL | End Of Line |
| EOT | End Of Transmission |

## F

| | |
|---|---|
| FAT | File Access Table |
| FCC | Federal Communications Commission |
| FCS | Frame Check Sequence |
| FDDI | Fiber Data Distributed Interface |
| FDM | Frequency Division Multiplexing |
| FT1 | Fractional T1 |
| FTAM | File Transfer Access and Management |
| FTP | File Transfer Protocol |

## G

| | |
|---|---|
| gated | Gateway Daemon |
| GB | Gigabyte |
| GGP | Gateway to Gateway Protocol |
| GHz | Gigahertz |
| GOSIP | Government OSI Profile |
| GUI | Graphical User Interface |

# H

| HDLC | High-level Data Link Control |
| HEMS | High-level Entity Management System |
| HMI | Hub Management Interface |
| HMP | Host Monitoring Protocol |
| HMS | Hub Management Services |
| HPFS | High Performance File System |
| Hz | Hertz |

# I

| IAB | Internet Activities Board |
| ICMP | Internet Control Message Protocol |
| IEEE | Institute of Electrical and Electronic Engineers |
| IEN | Internet Engineering Notes |
| IETF | Internet Engineering Task Force |
| IGMP | Internet Group Multicast Protocol |
| IGP | Interior Gateway Protocol |
| IMP | Interface Message Processor |
| INOC | Internet Network Operations Center |
| I/O | Input/Output |
| IP | Internet Protocol |
| IPC | Interprocess Communications Protocol |

| | |
|---|---|
| IPX | Internetwork Packet Exchange |
| IR | Internet Router |
| IRTP | Internet Reliable Transfer Protocol |
| ISA | Industry Standard Architecture |
| ISDN | Integrated Services Digital Network |
| ISO | International Organization for Standardization |
| IXC | Inter-Exchange Carrier |

# K

| | |
|---|---|
| Kbps | Kilo Bits per Second |
| KHz | Kilohertz |

# L

| | |
|---|---|
| LAN | Local Area Network |
| LAT | Local Area Transport |
| LATA | Local Area Transport Area |
| LAVC | Local Area VAX Cluster |
| LEC | Local Exchange Carrier |
| LLC | Logical Link Control |
| LMMP | LAN Man Management Protocol |
| LSL | Link Support Layer |

# M

| | |
|---|---|
| MAC | Media Access Control |
| MAN | Metropolitan Area Network |
| MAP | Manufacturing Automation Protocol |
| Mbps | Mega Bits per Second |
| MCA | Micro Channel Architecture |
| MHS | Message Handling Service |
| MHz | Megahertz |
| MIB | Management Information Base |
| MIPS | Millions Instructions Per Second |
| MIS | Management Information Systems |
| MILNET | MILitary NETwork |
| MLID | Multiple Link Interface Driver |
| MNP | Microcom Networking Protocol |
| MSAU | Multistation Access Unit |
| MTBF | Mean Time Between Failure |
| MTTR | Mean Time To Repair |
| MTU | Maximum Transmission Unit |
| MUX | Multiplex or Multiplexor |

# N

| | |
|---|---|
| NACS | NetWare Asynchronous Communications Services |
| NAK | Negative Acknowledgment |
| NASI | NetWare Asynchronous Service Interface |
| NAU | Network Addressable Unit |
| NAUN | Nearest Active Upstream Neighbor |
| NBP | Name Binding Protocol |
| NCP | Network Control Program |
| NCP | NetWare Core Protocol |
| NCSI | Network Communications Services Interface |
| NDIS | Network Driver Interface Standard |
| NDS | NetWare Directory Services |
| NetBEUI | NetBIOS Extended User Interface |
| NETBLT | Network Block Transfer |
| NetBIOS | Network Basic Input/Output System |
| NFS | Network File System |
| NIC | Network Interface Card |
| NIS | Network Information Services |
| NISC | Network Information Systems Center |

| | |
|---|---|
| NLM | NetWare Loadable Module |
| NMS | NetWare Management System |
| NNTP | Network News Transport Protocol |
| NOC | Network Operations Center |
| NOS | Network Operating System |
| NSF | National Science Foundation |
| NSFnet | National Science Foundation Network |

# O

| | |
|---|---|
| ODI | Open Data Link Interface |
| OS | Operating System |
| OSI | Open Systems Interconnect |
| OSPF | Open Shortest Path First |
| OUI | Organizationally Unique Identifiers |

# P

| | |
|---|---|
| PABX | Private Automatic Branch Exchange |
| PAD | Packet Assembler and Disassembler |
| PBX | Private Branch Exchange |
| PCM | Pulse Code Modulation |
| PDN | Public Data Network |
| PEP | Packet Exchange Protocol |

| | |
|---|---|
| PING | Packet InterNet Groper |
| POP | Point Of Presence |
| POP | Post Office Protocol |
| POSIX | Portable Operating System Interface - UNIX |
| PPP | Point-to-Point Protocol |
| PSN | Packet Switched Network |
| PSPDN | Packet Switched Public Data Network |
| PTP | Point-To-Point |
| PUC | Public Utilities Commission |
| PUP | PARC Universal Packet |

# R

| | |
|---|---|
| RAID | Redundant Array of Inexpensive Disks |
| RARP | Reverse Address Resolution Protocol |
| RDP | Reliable Datagram Protocol |
| RFC | Request For Comment |
| RIP | Routing Information Protocol |
| RISC | Reduced Instruction Set Computing |
| RJE | Remote Job Entry |
| RPC | Remote Procedure Calls |
| RTMP | Routing Table Maintenance Protocol |
| RTT | Round Trip Time |

APPENDIX D                                      *Abbreviations and Acronyms*

# S

| | |
|---|---|
| SAA | System Application Architecture |
| SACK | Selective Acknowledgment |
| SAP | Service Access Point |
| SCS | Systems Communications Services |
| SDLC | Synchronous Data Link Control |
| SIMM | Single In-Line Memory Module |
| SIPP | Single In-Line Pin Package |
| SLIP | Serial Line Internet Protocol |
| SMB | Server Message Block |
| SMDS | Switched Multimegabit Data Service |
| SMF | Standard Message Format |
| SMTP | Simple Mail Transfer Protocol |
| SNA | System Network Architecture |
| SNADS | Systems Network Architecture Distribution Services |
| SNAP | Sub-Network Access Protocol |
| SNMP | Simple Network Management Protocol |
| SOH | Start Of Header |
| SONET | Synchronous Optical Network |
| SPP | Sequenced Packet Protocol |
| SPX | Sequenced Packet Exchange |

| | |
|---|---|
| SQL | Structured Query Language |
| SR | Source Routing |
| SUT | Station Under Test |
| SYN | Synchronizing Segment |

# T

| | |
|---|---|
| TAC | Terminal Access Controller |
| TB | Terabyte |
| TCP | Transmission Control Protocol |
| TCP/IP | Transmission Control Protocol/Internet Protocol |
| TDM | Time Division Multiplexing |
| TDMA | Time Division Multiple Access |
| TDR | Time Domain Reflectometer |
| TELNET | TELecommunications NETwork |
| TFTP | Trivial File Transfer Protocol |
| TLI | Transport Layer Interface |
| TSR | Terminate and Stay Resident |
| TTL | Time To Live |

# U

| | |
|---|---|
| UART | Universal Asynchronous Receiver/Transmitter |
| UDP | User Datagram Protocol |

| | |
|---|---|
| UPS | Uninterruptible Power Supply |
| UTP | Unshielded Twisted Pair |
| UUCP | UNIX to UNIX Copy Program |

## V

| | |
|---|---|
| VAN | Value Added Network |
| VAP | Value Added Process |
| VGA | Video Graphics Array |
| VINES | Virtual Networking System |
| VLSI | Very Large Scale Integration |
| VMS | Virtual Memory System |
| VMTP | Versatile Message Transaction Protocol |

## W

| | |
|---|---|
| WAN | Wide Area Network |
| WANIS | Wide Area Network Interface Specification |
| WORM | Write Once Read Many |

## X

| | |
|---|---|
| XCVR | Transceiver |
| XDR | External Data Representation |
| XID | Exchange Identification |
| XNS | Xerox Network System |

# Y

YP  Yellow Pages (Replaced with NIS after legal dispute.)

# Z

ZIP  Zone Information Protocol
ZIT  Zone Information Table

# Appendix E

# Other Sources of Information

There are several places to get more information with regard to Ethernet and networking in general. I have listed some of these resources below. I would greatly encourage you to do plenty of independent research. It is not necessarily important that you fully understand all that you will find. Your familiarity with terms, acronyms, buzzwords, and phrases will, without a doubt, prove useful to you in the future.

| | |
|---|---|
| Ethernet version 2 standard, also known as the DIX standard or the Blue Book | DEC Direct (800) 344-4825 Part # AA-K759B-TK |
| IEEE 802.3 Standard (Inside the US and Canada) (Outside the US and Canada) | (800) 678-IEEE (908) 981-1393 (908) 981-9667 FAX |

| APPENDIX E | Other Sources of Information |
|---|---|

IEEE
445 Hoes Lane
PO Box 1311
Piscataway NJ 08855-1331
http://www.ieee.org/

TIA/EIA 568A and 568B        Global Engineering Documents
Cabling Standards            15 Iverness Way East
                             Englewood CO 80112
                             854-7179 (Inside the US)
                             (800) 387-4408 (Inside Canada)
                             397-7956 (Outside the US and Canada)
                             http://www.eia.org
                             http://www industry.net/tia

*Handbook of Computer-Communications Standards, Volume 1*
*The Open System (OSI) Model and OSI Related Standards,*
Vol. 1, Dr. William Stallings
Macmillan Publishing
ISBN: 0-02-415521-7

One chapter is dedicated to each layer. This is an excellent book to gain understanding of the functional aspects of the OSI model.

# Glossary

## A

### Application Layer

Layer 7 of the OSI model. This is where application programs such as databases are interfaced into the OSI model.

### AUI Cable

Attachment Unit Interface cable. This cable is most often used to attach devices, such as workstations, to transceivers. It is commonly called a transceiver cable.

## B

### Bandwidth

A measurement of capacity. For example, the data rate of Fast Ethernet is 100 megabits per second. If 50 million bits of information are being transmitted every second, then the remaining bandwidth is 50 percent.

*GLOSSARY*

### Baseband

The method of transmission where the cable is used to transmit a single signal.

### bit

Contraction of binary digit. This is the smallest unit of information. This unit may contain a value of one or zero.

### BNC

The most common opinion states that BNC stands for Bayonet-Neill-Concelman. This connector is a bayonet-locking type connector for coax.

### Broadband

The method of transmission where a single medium is used to transmit multiple signals simultaneously, without interference. An example would be cable TV, where many channels are brought to the television on a single coax cable.

### Broadcast

A function implemented in either hardware or software, which delivers a copy of a specified packet to all hosts attached to the same physical network and are enabled to receive broadcast data.

## Bus

A networking topology in which all of the nodes are connected to a single cable.

## Byte

Eight consecutive bits.

# C

## Checksum

A method used for detecting errors caused during the transmission of data. A calculation is made based on the data and the result is typically attached at the end of the transmission. Upon receipt of the transmission, the receiver applies a complementary calculation and compares the result against the transmitted checksum. If these do not match, a checksum error is generated.

## Collision

When two or more nodes attempt to transmit simultaneously on an Ethernet LAN.

*GLOSSARY*

## CRC

Cyclic Redundancy Check. A method of error detection. Using a standard algorithm, which performs a calculation on the packet, the transmitting station generates a number, which is in turn inserted into the transmitted packet. When the receiving station receives the packet, the algorithm is applied again and the new number is compared against the transmitted number. A match indicates that the data was received as sent. A mismatch indicates a data transmission error.

## CSMA

Carrier Sense Multiple Access. Allows multiple nodes attached to a single transmission medium to contend for access by sensing a period of idle time on the medium.

## CSMA/CD

Carrier Sense Multiple Access with Collision Detection. An implementation of CSMA with the ability to detect simultaneous transmission of two or more nodes. This is the basis of IEEE 802.3 specification.

## Current-Mode Transmission

Current is sent is opposite directions on either of two conductors depending on the binary value being transmitted.

# D

## *Data Link Layer*

The second layer in the OSI model. This layer takes care of establishing and releasing connections.

# F

## *File Server*

A computer system that provides file access via a LAN for multiple users.

## *Full Duplex Mode*

Full-Duplex is a transmission mode that allows transmission to occur in both directions simultaneously.

# H

## *Half-Duplex Mode*

Half-Duplex is a transmission mode that allows transmission of data in both directions but only one at a time.

GLOSSARY

### *Heartbeat*
*See* SQE.

# I

### *IEEE 802.3*
A physical layer standard using CSMA/CD on a bus topology.

# J

### *Jabber*
When a node fails and continuously transmits.

# L

### *LAN*
Local Area Network. The network is said to be local when it is confined to a restricted geographical area. A LAN may have gateways to Wide Area Networks or other public or private LANs.

# M

## *Media Access Unit*

Often referred to as a transceiver. The most common application used to be running transceiver cables from a thick coax spine to individual systems. However, there are transceivers to convert to an AUI cable from thin coax, twisted pair and fiber as well.

# N

## *Network Layer*

The third layer of the OSI model. The task of the network layer is to provide network addresses and service selection. This is where the IP (Internet Protocol) of TCP/IP is found.

## *Node*

Any device attached to the network, usually a computer.

# P

## *Physical Layer*

The first Layer of the OSI model. The physical layer provides the mechanical and electrical connection and control function. The elements in this layer include transceivers and Ethernet controllers.

GLOSSARY

## Presentation Layer

The sixth Layer of the OSI model. This layer is responsible for transferring information from the application to the operating system.

# R

## Repeater

A device that repeats a signal. The basic repeater connects two segments of Ethernet within the same LAN together. Any signal from either segment is received by the repeater and the signal is then retransmitted by the repeater to both segments. The repeater also performs collision checking.

# T

## Topology

The specific geometric or logical shape of a network configuration. The most common are bus, star, and ring.

# W

## WAN

Wide Area Network. A network that spans beyond the reach of a LAN. A WAN covers the distance between buildings, cities, states, and countries.

# Index

10BASE-
 2, 45
 5, 45, 50
 F, 45
 T, 45
100BASE-FX, 45, 65
100BASE-T, 59
100BASE-X, 64
8B6T, 64

## A

Application Layer, 12
ATM, 17
Attachment Unit Interface, *See* AUI
AUI, 33, 50, 51, 97
Auto-negotiation, 67

## B

broadcast address, 36, 42
Bus, 6

## C

carrier, 20
 sense, 20
 Sense Multiple Access with Collision Detection, *See* CSMA/CD
Client Layer protocol, 36
Collision, 20
 detection, 20
 Presence Signal, *See* CPS
CPS, 33
CSMA/CD, 19, 21, 46, 57, 73

*INDEX*

## D

data field, 36, 40
Data Link Layer, 12, 32
Data Terminal Equipment, 50
destination address, 35, 39, 42
DIX, 97
DTE, 50, 51, 122

## E

EIA, 3
Electronic Industry Association, *See* EIA
Ethernet, 17, 18;
    benefits of, 22
    version 1, 29
    version 2 frame, 33

## F

Fast Ethernet, 58, 69
FDDI, 17
frame(s), 19
    check sequence, 36, 40

## I

IEEE, 18
    488 standard, 6
    802.3 standard, 19, 37, 45
Institute of Electrical and Electronic Engineers, *See* IEEE
International Organization for Standardization, *See* ISO
ISO, 11, 14

## J

jam signal, 21

## L

LAN, 1, 10, 14, 19
length field, 40
Local Area Network, *See* LAN

# M

MAC, 19, 47, 60, 71
MAU, 60
MDI, 50
Media Access Control, *See* MAC
Medium
  Attachment Unit, *See* MAU
  Dependent Interface, *See* MDI
  Independent Interface, *See* MII
MII, 60, 64, 69, 71
multicast
  address, 35, 42
  group address, 35
multiple access, 20

# N

network(s), 2, 15
  interface card (NIC), 22
  Layer, 12

# O

Open Systems Interconnect (OSI), 11, 13, 14

# P

PCS, 64
PHY, 60
Physical address, 35, 42
  Layer, 12, 32
  Layer Entity, *See* PHY
  Media Dependent, *See* PMD
PMA, 64, 70
PMD, 65
preamble, 35, 39
Presentation Layer, 12

# R

Ring, 5

*INDEX*

## S

sense, 20
Session Layer, 12
Signal Quality Error, *See* SQE
source address, 36, 39
SQE, 37, 70
Star, 7
start frame delimiter field, 39

## T

Token Ring, 17
Topology, 15
Transport Layer, 12
type field, 36

## U

Unshielded Twisted Pair, 95, 103

## W

Wide Area Networks (WANs), 10, 15

## X

X.25, 17